D1236542

The Loyalist Corps

Americans in
the Service of
the King

Thomas B. Allen • Todd W. Braisted

The Loyalist Corps: Americans in the Service of the King

Print Edition ISBN 0-9818487-8-8
ISBN-13: 978-0-9818487-8-5

Takoma Park • Maryland
FoxAcre.com

Table of Contents

The Armed Loyalists

King George III

by Thomas B. Allen

Loyalists fought in more than 150 military units that were raised during the Revolutionary War. In the South alone, British military archives list 26 units that fought during southern campaigns.

Most British Army regiments had long, well-documented, and respected histories. Loyalist units, however, came and went, dissolving or merging over the course of the war and leaving scant records behind. When the war ended, the British Army would live on, while the Loyalist Provincial Corps, as the British called the Tory units, would fade away.

These descriptions of Loyalist military units in many ways reflect the complicated and often uncertain histories of the units themselves. Records are spotty, primarily because the British Army, a great keeper of records, did not regard their Loyalist comrades as equals. The Crown did not award battle honors to British regiments that fought in America because the British saw the Revolution as a civil war. Intercine fights did not rate such honors. (Battle honors were, however, awarded for actions

9

against America's French and Spanish allies in the West Indies and other theatres.)

More than 1,500 Americans became Loyalist officers. Their success at recruiting produced unexpected results. Regular British Army officers, whose commissions almost inevitably stemmed from wealth and family connections, resented the Loyalist officers easily acquired commissions and promotions,

The better the Loyalist officers were at talking and promising, the quicker they formed regiments and the faster came their captaincies and colonelcies. Regiments were often formed not on the basis of military wisdom or experience but also on the ability of recruiters to get men to sign up for specific periods of time. Regulars, as professional officers, kept track of their careers, not their calendars.

Unlike British and Hessian troops, Loyalist soldiers went into battle knowing that if they were captured they would most likely be treated as criminals—not as prisoners of war. They may have thought of themselves as Loyalists allied to British forces. But to the Rebels they were Tories, who, in the words of a New York law, were to be "treated as open enemies." All the states passed anti-Tory laws with penalties ranging from exile to execution. (See "Punishing the Tories" at www. toriesfightingfortheking.com)

Thousands of Loyalist soldiers were in the army that British General Lieutenant General John Burgoyne led in his campaign to conquer New York and seal off the state from New England. When Burgoyne's offensive ended in defeat at Saratoga in October 1777, he managed to save many American Loyalists by calling them Canadians. Under the "Saratoga Convention," neither they nor British and Hessian troops were called prisoners of war.

The Convention was Burgoyne's name for the agreement between him and the Continental Army commander, Major General Horatio Gates. The Convention called for the British and Hessian troops to be marched to Boston, where they would board British ships and sail to England, never to fight in America again. The Loyalists who trekked to Canada, because they were covered by the Convention, agreed not to take up arms again.

When the Continental Congress abrogated the Convention, the captives who had been marched to Massachusetts became prisoners of war and were eventually put in prison camps in Virginia, Maryland, and Pennsylvania. The Loyalists in Canada, known as Convention of Saratoga prisoners, declared themselves no longer under the Convention because Congress had abolished the agreement. Many of these Convention Loyalists then returned to America and resumed fighting.

• • •

A number of Loyalist units came and went very quickly. They usually consisted of twenty or even fewer men who were assigned to garrison duty, police patrols, digging fortifications, cutting wood, guarding woodcutting parties, and other routine duties. They left behind little record of what they had done.

Many smaller units were eventually merged into larger units. These were often called "Independent Corps" or "Independent Companies," and many saw significant combat and fought valiantly.

Adding to the confusion, many units were known by more than one name–or even two or three similar names. Such units are listed in the Roster of Units on these pages by what appears to be the primary name, with alternate names listed immediately below. These alternate names are included in the index in the print edition of this volume.

A unit's name was not always a reliable guide to where the unit was raised. For example, the Jamaica Corps was raised in Charleston. Many units were raised in one locale and transported to another. The Maryland Loyalists fought in Florida, were all taken prisoner and shipped to Cuba (a possession of Spain, which had joined France as an American ally). From Cuba, the

Marylanders went to New York. At the end of war, while sailing for Canada, most of them died in a shipwreck.

Several units recruited free blacks and escaped slaves who were offered their freedom in exchange for serving the Loyalist cause. Officers of such units were white, but the ranks of some included whites. These units did some fighting, but more typically served as "Pioneers," a term that in this context means doing the digging, cleaning, and other less glamorous military tasks.

Many reports describe the drafting of one unit into another. In effect, this meant that the unit was disbanded, with its soldiers and officers being placed in the receiving unit. A unit might even be drafted into two or more receiving units. This might happen if morale had collapsed in a unit, if the unit had simply lost too many men to disease, war wounds, and desertion, or if, from an administrative point of view, the unit was simply too small to bother with.

It is also important to view the war from a British, imperial point of view. The King's generals did not see the thirteen rebellious colonies as being especially different from the other British colonies in the western hemisphere. Troops might be moved back and forth between Canada, Bermuda, Jamaica, Georgia or New York as needed. Troops recruited to fight the Continental Army might be sent to deal with a Spanish challenge in Florida, or vice versa. The western Atlantic, the Gulf of Mexico, and the coastal regions of North America, from Newfoundland to Central America were all part of one vast theater of operations, with units deployed as far away as present-day Nicaragua. Troops, ships, and supplies were shifted from one place to another as needed. Thus, a force raised in Jamaica was seen as not much different from one raised in New Jersey. The men in both were provincial soldiers, in the service of the King.

For the most part, we have presented the units in alphabetical order by name. However, where the units were closely linked to each other operationally or where it otherwise seemed to make more sense to group the units from certain colonies together, we have done so.

• • •

An initial draft of the unit descriptions was compiled by my son, Roger MacBride Allen. This work was done in conjunction with the preparation of my book *Tories: Fighting for the King in America's First Civil War.* A briefer listing of Loyalist military units, along with much other information about the Loyalists, appears at the website for that book, www. toriesfightingfortheking.com

Todd W. Braisted's On-Line Institute for Advanced Loyalist Studies (see www.royalprovincial.com) was a primary source for the initial draft of the present book, which was then updated, corrected, and expanded by Mr. Braisted.

Additional sources used include books and resources available to the general public: *American Loyalist Troops 1775-84* by René Chartand, Osprey Publishing, Ltd. 2008; *The American Provincial Corps* 1775-84 by Philip Katcher and Michael Youens, Osprey Publishing, Ltd., 1973; Stefan Bielinski's Colonial Albany Social History Project (www.nysm.nysed.gov/albany/); The Loyalist Gazette (www.uelac.org/publications. php#gazette); and The King's Men (www.nyhistory.net/). Just as this book was nearing completion, the encyclopedic reference volume *Military Loyalist of the American Revolution: Officers and Regiments, 1775-1783* by Walter T. Dornfest was released.

The Loyalist Corps

by Todd W. Braisted

The Loyalist equivalent of the Continental Army was referred to as the Provincial Corps. Raised under the auspices of the commander in chief of the British Army, in all theaters of the conflict, these troops were enlisted for the duration of the war and liable for service anywhere in North America. They received the same pay, provisions, quality of clothing, arms, equipage, and accoutrements as British soldiers, while serving under the same discipline. Some units were short-lived and some served for the whole war.

Numerous British officers and sergeants were sprinkled throughout these units to help bring them up to a state of tactical proficiency and professionalism. Provincial units were primarily used in limited roles early in the war, but as the number of British units dwindled in America, the value of the Provincial units increased, taking a leading part, particularly in the South. When units became significantly under-strength, with little prospect of recruiting anew, members of those units were generally drafted into other regiments.

Five Provincial regiments received the special status of being placed on what the British Army called the "American Establishment." This was considered an honor, given to units that had achieved their recruiting goals or performed particularly well in battle. Not coincidentally, current or former British officers commanded four of these five units. Seven Provincial units, including three on the American Establishment, achieved the highest recognition by being placed upon the Regular Establishment.

Some Loyalist units were raised by order of the governor of a province, if the British government functioned there. These were standing corps, paid for and supplied through the governor's budget. These units were not a part of the army per se, and did not enjoy the same benefits as Provincial troops. Most served only a limited time and all were disbanded before the end of the war. Such units included the West Florida Provincials, the East Florida Rangers, and the Ethiopian Regiment. These were the equivalent of the so-called State Troops raised from time to time by the states.

Militia laws were either in place or passed wherever the Crown held sway. Under these laws, the militia generally consisted of all able-bodied males between the ages of sixteen and sixty, usually with exemptions for Quakers, firemen, and the civil authorities. These units were typically raised along county lines and only served when needed. Some of these militia corps were volunteers, while others were compulsory. The volunteer units were often uniformed, while the other corps mostly provided their own arms, ammunition, equipage, and clothing.

Militia men on active service generally drew British provisions—and sometimes British Army pay. This confirmed the rank of officers in the army as well as guaranteed them half-pay upon retirement, known in the British Army as "reduction."

The militias primarily acted on the orders of a province's governor, as in Georgia, Nova Scotia, and New York. British military commanders took a much more active role in directing the activities of militias in the Carolinas.

The least structured units tended to be those under the appellation of "Associators" or "Refugees." These tended to be separate and distinct from the army, tailoring their operations to achieve self-interests or financial gains. One of them, the Associated Loyalists, operated under a charter from the king himself. The Loyal Associated Refugees not only lived by "interrupting commerce" as privateers but also by contracting to perform such work as collecting wood from inhabitants of Martha's Vineyard. These units received minimal support from the British, and their near-autonomy was a source of some friction with different British commanders.

The following military units described here were more or less raised through official means and were regularly supplied with men. Temporary formations were often created as the exigency of the situation required, such as temporary militia companies formed at Savannah and Yorktown during their respective sieges. Militia units were likewise occasionally formed by local army commanders in Georgia and the Carolinas, and these units sometimes quickly passed into history. The militias throughout the Province of Quebec were more regularly organized, but they had scant active military roles.

A large number of Loyalists served in both the Civil Branches of the Army and Artillery. These organizations were the support services of the military, employing wagoners, laborers, and skilled mechanics. Thousands served in their ranks, in all theaters of the war.

A few Loyalists, such as Oliver DeLancey, Jr., and Arent Schuyler DePeyster, were officers or enlisted soldiers in Regular British regiments. More served in the Royal Navy, some by voluntary enlistment, others the results of impressment. Thousands additionally took to the seas in privately owned and armed warships, known as letters of marque or privateers. These ships, usually built for speed over heavy firepower, were engaged in attacks on enemy commerce, with the prize vessels and cargoes sold for the benefit of both the owners and crew.

Loyalists willing to risk their lives served as spies, army guides, or ship pilots. The Indian Department employed many

Loyalists and occasionally had in it such units as Brant's Volunteers or the Loyal Foresters.

One of the most distinguished and prominent Loyalist units, made up mostly of New Yorkers, was the King's American Regiment, led by Colonel Edmund Fanning. The regiment served in six major campaigns across the length of the eastern seaboard. The officers and men fought in some of the bloodiest battles of the war, ending their service by being placed on the regular British Establishment, an honor bestowed on but a handful of Loyalist units.

A Note on Sources

The search for all the Loyalist organizations that took part in the America War for Independence has taken me to Canada, the United Kingdom and throughout here in the United States. The British Army at the commencement of the war consisted of 70 regiments of infantry, along with artillery, cavalry and the Guards. As in previous conflicts, the army would expand by increasing its own ranks, hiring troops from the different German principalities, and raising new corps in the colonies. It is a brief listing of the latter that is the subject of this work.

Finding the who and what of Loyalist units was no easy task. Many men of influence attempted to raise corps of all sorts, be they Provincials, militia, refugees, etc. Many of these corps failed to raise they number of men required to justify their existence, forcing many consolidations prior to the end of the war. Many units were only raised when the British Army arrived in a particular geographic area and was able to supply clothing, arms, pay, provisions, etc. The records of these corps exist today, in varying degrees of completeness, and by using them do we get an accurate picture of the extent and scope of England's colonial troops.

In the United Kingdom, the two main repositories consulted were The National Archives (TNA) and the British Library. In these places lay thousands of manuscript documents telling the broad story of the war and many individual tales. TNA sources consulted over the course of several decades include Audit Office, Colonial Office, War Office, Treasury, Treasury Solicitor, Chancery, Home Office, Admiralty, Foreign Office, Cornwallis Papers and Carleton Papers. Everything from correspondence to muster rolls, memorials, courts martial, pension applications, returns, orders, etc. may be found amongst those collections. The British Library is the home of the Additional Manuscripts, amongst which is the Haldimand Papers, providing a treasure trove of information on the Northern Army. Other institutions providing information in the UK include the Royal Artillery Institute, the Scottish Record Office, Alnwick Castle and Ballindolloch Castle.

Canada, which provided a place of refuge for thousands of Loyalists after the war, today houses excellent records of units, particularly those in the Provincial line. Library and Archives Canada in Ottawa contains hundreds of Provincial muster rolls in the Chipman Papers and RG 8 Series. Collections such as the Nairne Family Papers and Malcolm Fraser Papers contain great information on the Northern Army, while the Upper Canada Land Petitions help sort out service and postwar settlement. The Provincial Archives in Newfoundland, New Brunswick, Nova Scotia and Ontario all have numerous collections. Of particular note in Nova Scotia is the Gideon White Papers, militia lists in RG 1, and last petitions in RG 20A. The Provincial Archives of New Brunswick has similar land documents but also numerous pension applications of Loyalist veterans. The University of New Brunswick contains the papers of the muster master general of Provincial Forces, Edward Winslow. Saint John's New Brunswick Museum also possesses some important muster rolls, journals and orderly books.

Gathering Loyalist research in the United States can be a daunting task, given the numerous institutions from coast to coast. Good sources, containing muster rolls, orderly books, correspondence, etc. can be found in the state historical societies of Maine, Massachusetts, New York, New Jersey, Pennsylvania, Delaware, Maryland, Virginia, South Carolina and Georgia. The state archives of Pennsylvania, New York and New Jersey, as well as the New York Public Library, contain numerous rolls, abstracts and other Loyalist military collections. California's Huntington Library has some significant material concerning correspondence and pay abstracts. Both the Library of Congress and the National Archives and Records Administration have material that can be mined for Loyalists, particularly the Peter Force Papers in the former, and the Papers of the Continental Congress and US Pension Applications at the latter. The University of Michigan's premiere research facility, the William L. Clements Library, has numerous manuscript collections chock full of Loyalist material, such as the Thomas Gage Papers, Sir Henry Clinton Papers, Sackville Germain Papers, Frederick Mackenzie Papers, John G. Simcoe Papers, and George Wray Papers.

However, for one-stop shopping on Loyalist collections, no institution can boast more material than the David Library of the American Revolution. Located in Washington Crossing, Pennsylvania, the library has microfilm of many of the key British, Canadian and American collections, as well as numerous newspapers. To them, and all the curators I owe a great deal of thanks over the years, as well as to my research colleagues Don Londahl-Smidt, Don Hagist, and Walter Dornfest.

For more information on many of the corps mentioned in this work, please visit my website, www.royalprovincial.com. The site contains selections of documents from many of the places mentioned above, and is intended to help guide people towards the collections and institutions that will assist them in their Loyalist studies. My thanks to Nan Cole and John Korchok for their time and dedication in helping make that site a reality.

Roster of Units

Adams Company of Rangers

An independent company raised for the British Army, this unit was founded by Capt. Samuel Adams, who lived in what is now Arlington, Vermont. Rebels once hoisted Adams, in an armchair, twenty-five feet to place him next to a stuffed catamount on a tavern sign pole in Bennington. Most of the unit's 70 men came from New York and New Hampshire Grants, the long-disputed territory that became Vermont. Raised during the Burgoyne Campaign, the corps was divided into two sections, one of Rangers, and one of batteau-men. About half the corps was present at the Convention of Saratoga, while the remainder successfully made their way to Canada. The unit was incorporated into McAlpin's Corps of Royalists in 1780.

American Legion

Raised by Benedict Arnold in October 1780, the Legion was meant to be formed from deserters of the Continental Army. The Legion, at its height, consisted of three troops of cavalry and six companies of infantry. A total of 475 officers and men served under Arnold, most notably during the Virginia expedition led by Arnold himself in 1781 and the raid on New London, Connecticut later that year. The corps was disbanded along the Saint John River on October 10, 1783.

Benedict Arnold in the uniform of
a Continental Army major general.
Drawn by Pierre Du Simitiere, New-York Historical Society.

American Volunteers
also known as Ferguson's Provincials

This was a temporary corps of 175 officers and men drawn from volunteers of the Provincial units at New York City who would not otherwise be a part of the campaign to take Charlestown, South Carolina. The corps providing the men included the 1st, 2nd and 4th Battalion of New Jersey Volunteers, the 3rd Battalion DeLancey's, the King's American Regiment, Loyal American Regiment, Prince of Wales American Volunteers and Nassau Blues. After the surrender of Charleston, the corps' commander, Patrick Ferguson, received permission to keep the unit in South

Carolina, where they were invaluable in training Loyalist militia in light infantry tactics. The 70 remaining Volunteers formed the core of the 1,000-man force that was nearly wiped out in the battle of King's Mountain on October 7, 1780. The survivors, in an exchange with captured Rebels, returned to their parent regiments the following year.

Patrick Ferguson
Anonymous miniature,
c. 1774-77, from a private
collection

Armed Boat Company

Authorized by Sir Henry Clinton in July 1781, this seagoing unit manned armed whaleboats (narrow vessels about thirty-six feet long, with pointed bows and sterns, sometimes armed with small cannon). Several members of the unit were former slaves. Among the unit's combat operations were attacks on Rebel whaleboats in New Brunswick, New Jersey, in January 1782 and an attack on a Rebel blockhouse at Tom's River, New Jersey, in March 1782. The unit was commanded by Capt. William Luce of New Jersey, and later Capt. Nathan Hubbell, formerly of the Associated Loyalists. The company continued to serve until the final evacuation of New York City in November 1783.

Artificer and Labourer Volunteers

One of three units raised by Capt. Robert Pringle, an officer in the British Corps of Engineers. He was in charge of constructing new defenses in the harbor of St. John's, Newfoundland, when the war began. This 115-man unit was raised in 1778 from amongst the Civil Branch of the Royal Artillery serving on the island. This was a temporary unit meant to supplement the island's small garrison until more troops were on hand.

Associated Loyalists

Created by Royal Charter in 1780, this organization was meant to combine political representation from the thirteen colonies along with an autonomous military arm, free to plan and execute their own operations and independent of the British military command. The military wing consisted of companies of "Associators" who were neither paid or uniformed by the British. The Associators would support themselves through the proceeds of prizes obtained during their excursions. The military wing answered to the Board of Associated Loyalists, headed by former New Jersey Governor William Franklin (estranged son of Benjamin Franklin) who authorized expeditions and regulated all other aspects of the Association. The corps operated primarily from Lloyd's Neck, Long Island, and Sandy Hook, New Jersey. The most infamous incident in its history occurred when one of its officers, Capt. Richard Lippencott (or Lippincott) of New Jersey, executed an officer of the New Jersey State Troops under his charge, Capt. Joshua Huddy, as an act of retaliation.

William Franklin
Detail of 1790 portrait
by Mather Brown

Lippencott was court-martialed for his action, but eventually found not guilty. The trial did have the affect of leading to the dissolving of the Association in 1782.

Bagaduce Regiment

Before the Revolution began, Thomas Goldthwait, a Boston merchant, served as Secretary of War for Massachusetts Bay. He was also commander of Fort Pownall, built in 1760 at the mouth of the Penobscot River (now in Maine, then part of Massachusetts). When British forces seized the fort's cannons and powder in 1775, Goldthwait was branded a traitor. As an admitted Tory, he formed and commanded the Bagaduce Regiment, named after a town later named Castine. He later fled to British-occupied New York City on a Royal Navy warship and eventually sailed to England, where he died in 1799. The corps consisted of the inhabitants of the Penobscot area, enrolled after the British occupied the area in 1779.

Barbadian Rangers

Raised in Barbados from July 1781 and intended for service in the Leeward Islands, the Rangers were commanded by Capt. Timothy Thornhill, a member of what was called the Barbados aristocracy of sugar and slaves. This 82-man light infantry company served primarily in Antigua.

Bay Fusiliers
also known as Mosquito Shore Volunteers and Black River Volunteers

Both free men and slaves belonged to this unit, raised and based on the Mosquito Coast of what is now Nicaragua and commanded by a British officer, Maj. James Lawrie. The Fusiliers were used in operations against forces of Spain, which had become an ally of France in 1779.

Bermuda Militia

By war's end, over 1,200 men in nine companies were enrolled in the island's militia, commanded by Col. Francis Jones.

Black Dragoons
also known as Black Pioneer Troop

This cavalry unit was the only all-black unit on the South Carolina Militia establishment. Raised in late 1781, it helped form a part of Lt. Col. Benjamin Thompson's cavalry corps outside of Charleston during that officer's brief stay in the province. Used primarily to intercept British deserters, the troop's history ended with evacuation of Charleston in December 1782.

Black Hussars
also known as Diemar's Hussars

This unit of black-coated troops was formed mainly of escaped German prisoners of war who had been captured during the Burgoyne Campaign. Organized as a temporary troop on the Provincial establishment, the hussars were commanded by Capt. Frederick De Diemar of the British 60th Regiment of Foot. They were attached at times to the British Legion or the Queen's American Rangers. They fought at such engagements as New Rochelle, Stanwick, Hopperstown, Connecticut Farms and Springfield. The troop officially became a part of the Queen's Rangers on April 25, 1781, where it was often referred to as the "German Troop."

Black Pioneers

Gen. Henry Clinton formed this unit during his expedition to North Carolina in 1776. The initial unit consisted of 71 escaped slaves, who were given their freedom and put under the command of Capt. George Martin, a lieutenant in the British Marines. They dug latrines, cleared ground to build camps, and did other such menial army chores. Although no Black Pioneer was killed in battle, many died of disease and overwork. New enlistments usually kept the size of the unit to no more than 50 to 60 men. The Black Pioneers were the only Loyalist unit to accompany Clinton in his attack on Newport, Rhode Island in December 1776. After returning to New York, the Black Pioneers in 1777 were sent to Philadelphia, where they were ordered to "Attend the Scavangers, Assist in Cleaning the Streets & Removing all Newsiances being threwn into the Streets." A second company, commanded by Capt. Robert Richard Crowe, which never got larger than 20 men, was disbanded in 1778. Another unit of Black Pioneers was raised during the siege of Savannah in September and October 1779. Black Pioneers would be among the last Loyalists to be evacuated from New York City in 1783. Like other Provincials, the company drew land in Nova Scotia, but their land was inferior to what was given to white Loyalists. The Pioneers' last commander was Capt. Allan Stewart of North Carolina, who would later command the North Carolina Highlanders.

Boston Regiment, Massachusetts Militia

The remnants of Boston's pre-war militia were still serving with the British in 1775, until superseded by the Loyal American Association later that year. In June 1775, at least some militia were serving as such under Capt. John Erving.

Brant's Volunteers

This small ad hoc group was led by the Mohawk Joseph Brant (Thayendanegea), who started the war as an assistant interpreter in the Indian Department. The Indian Department was the branch of the British military assigned to work with native tribes, cultivate their friendship, and coordinate military activity

Joseph Brant was painted by Gilbert Stuart in 1786 when he was in London Collection of the Duke of Northumberland.

during time of war. Unlike a military regiment, the department was composed primarily of officers, many from standing British regiments, along with interpreters, artificers and a small number of rangers. Brant was one who took up arms at a time when many tribes stood idle. This independent spirit continued during the war, drawing to himself those who wished to work outside the system. Brant, finally elevated in 1779 by Lt. Gen. Frederick Haldimand to captain in the Indian Department, would go on to lead numerous raids along the Pennsylvania/New York/New Jersey frontier, the most successful of which was the total defeat of militia at the battle of Minisink, July 22, 1779. By the end of the war, Brant's Volunteers, fifteen men and their families, were a part of the Indian Department serving at Niagara.

British Legion
also known as 5th American Regiment and Tarleton's Legion

Formed in 1778 by merging the Philadelphia Light Dragoons, Caledonian Volunteers, and Kinloch's Light Dragoons, along with drafts from the Roman Catholic Volunteers, Royal American Reformees, West Jersey Volunteers and others. On

December 25, 1779 the unit absorbed the Bucks County Light Dragoons. Many of the units' recruits came from Pennsylvania, New York and New Jersey. The corps took part in numerous skirmishes in Westchester, capturing the colors of the 2nd Light Dragoons at Pound Ridge in July 1779. They fought in battles in the Southern campaign at Monck's Corner, Waxhaws, Fishing Creek, Cowpens, Guilford Courthouse, Camden, Blackstocks, and Charlottesville. The corps surrendered with the army at Yorktown on October 19, 1781. The Legion was raised by Col. Lord Cathcart, a captain in the British 17th Light Dragoons. After Cathcart's resignation from Provincial command, the corps was taken over by its lieutenant colonel, Banastre Tarleton, a brilliant

Colonel Banastre Tarleton, in a portrait by Sir Joshua Reynolds, stands on Rebel battle flags heaped at his feet. On Flag Day 2006 an anonymous bidder paid nearly $17.4 million for four rare flags captured by Tarleton in the American Revolution. A flag he captured at Pound Ridge, New York, is one of the first to display the 13 red and white stripes, and a flag he captured in South Carolina is one of the first to display 13 five-pointed stars on a field of blue. National Gallery, London

British Army career officer who, early in the war, assisted in the capture of Continental Army Gen. Charles Lee. In 1781 it was put on the American Establishment as the 5th American Regiment. On December 25, 1782 the cavalry of the corps was made a regular regiment of the British Army. The corps was disbanded in Nova Scotia on October 10, 1783.

Bucks County Light Dragoons
also known as Bucks County Dragoons

Raised in Philadelphia in April 1778, the unit took part in the battle of Monmouth, and attached to the Queen's Rangers for the 1779 campaign, when it joined the cavalry of that unit in the raid on Somerset. The troop was made a part of the British Legion on December 25, 1779. Lt. Col. John Watson Tadswell Watson, a British Army officer from the elite Brigade of Guards, led the dragoons after the regular commander, Capt. Thomas Sandford, was taken prisoner. Capt. Sandford resumed his command upon being exchanged in 1779.

Bucks County Volunteers

Raised in the spring of 1778 under Capt. William Thomas, the unit may have had as few as 15 to 20 men at times and was often attached to the Queen's Rangers. This was not a Provincial unit, but rather a volunteer company in every sense of the word, serving without pay, uniforms, etc. The company consisted of eighty men at the time of the evacuation of Philadelphia. Prior to the evacuation, the company fought at Jenk's Mills, Smithfield and Frankfort.

Butler's Rangers

One of the most effective Provincial units raised, and the one most closely associated in working with England's Indian allies in America. Authorized by Sir Guy Carleton on September 15, 1777 "to serve with the Indians, as occasion shall require," the corps was raised by Maj., later Lt. Col., John Butler, the deputy agent in the Indian Department serving at Niagara. It was from there that the corps would be headquartered and serve for the next seven years. Fighting on their own, and with the Indians or alongside other Provincial and British units, the corps took part in some of the most brutal fighting of the war. About 200 Rangers and 300 Indians raided Wyoming Valley, Pennsylvania, in June 1778. They continued to raid the New York frontier throughout the war. During a raid into Cherry Valley, New York, Butler's Indian allies killed unarmed men, women and children. One company was sent to Detroit and raided Rebel settlements along the western frontier. In the final Ranger action of the war, one company raided and torched Wheeling in today's West Virginia. During their peak years the Rangers mustered more than 500 men. Butler's son Walter, an ensign in the British King's (or 8th)

John Butler
Niagara Historical Society &
Museum

Regiment, became a captain in the Rangers. He was killed at the battle of West Canada Creek on October 30, 1781. By the end of the war, more than 900 men had served in the Rangers. While the bulk of the corps was discharged on 24 June 1784, one company became the last Provincials still in service, not being disbanded until July 16, 1784. The corps would receive their grants of land in the new province of Upper Canada.

Caledonian Volunteers

Raised in Philadelphia and New York in 1778, the unit was merged with the British Legion on their formation in July of that year, after reaching a strength of about eighty men. The commander was Lt. Col. William Sutherland, who was with the British soldiers at the North Bridge in Concord when "the shot heard round the world" began the Revolutionary War.

Canadian Companies

Canadian referred to French-speaking Canadians, who were reluctant to get involved in the fight between the British and the Americans. The British believed the Canadians would be the first to join their efforts in quelling the rebellion, and authorized the raising of 6,000 men. In the end, only three companies of about 100 men each would be raised. The 1st company was raised from the Trois-Rivières district, the 2nd from around Montreal, the 3rd from Quebec. The 1st company served at the failed siege of Fort Stanwix, New York, during the Burgoyne Campaign. The 2nd and 3rd marched with Burgoyne and were part of the "Convention Army" that surrendered at Saratoga. Company officers were Capt. Samuel Mackay, Capt. Jean-Baptiste-Melchior Hertel De Rouville, Capt. David Monin, Lt. Jean-Baptiste Beaubien, and Capt. René-Amable Boucher de Boucherville. The Canadian Companies were disbanded after the 1777 campaign, although the officers remained upon full pay after the unit was disbanded.

Carolina Black Corps
also known as Carolina Corps, Black Carolina Corps, Black Corps of Dragoons Pioneers and Artificers

This black unit was raised as the British Army was leaving Charleston in December 1782. After the Revolution, the corps of former slaves, amalgamated into a single unit called the Black Carolina Corps, served in British Caribbean possessions, which were slave states until slavery was officially abolished in most of the British Empire on August 1, 1834. The unit was commanded by Col. John Montagu Mainwaring throughout most of its history, serving late into the 1790's.

Charlestown, South Carolina Militia

Organized after the fall of this city in 1780 to the British, it consisted at first of one battalion, commanded by Col. Robert William Powell. A second battalion was added in 1781, commanded by Lt. Col. Thomas Inglis. The battalions were uniformed and included companies of grenadiers. The corps served until the evacuation of the city in 1782.

Charlestown Volunteer Battalion

Formed at the request of some of the inhabitants of Charleston, this light infantry militia corps was commanded by Maj. James Buchannon. It performed routine garrison duty until disbanded at the evacuation of the city in December 1782.

Collett's Independent Company of Provincials

Raised in the winter of 1776-1777 by Capt. John Collett, a former officer in the Queen's Own Loyal Virginia Regiment. The company was made a part of the Prince of Wales' American Volunteers on April 4, 1777.

DeLancey's Brigade

Amongst the first Provincial units raised on the British Army's arrival at New York was a brigade of three battalions commanded by one of the province's leading Loyalists, Oliver DeLancey. Commissioned a brigadier general on September 4, 1776, DeLancey recruited some 2,000 officers and men primarily from

Long Island and Connecticut. Due to severe losses in the 2nd Battalion, it was drafted into the 1st on February 24, 1782. At that time the 3rd was renumbered as a new 2nd Battalion.

1st Battalion, DeLancey's Brigade

Commanded by Lt. Col. John Harris Cruger, one member of His Majesty's Council for New York and a prominent merchant in New York City. Stationed primarily on Long Island until the end of 1778, they took part in several skirmishes, including the loss of forty men at Sag Harbor in 1777 to Gen. Meigs. In November 1778 the battalion accompanied Lt. Col. Archibald Campbell's expedition to take Savannah, with men of the battalion also fighting at Briar Creek and, Stono Ferry in 1779. After the successful defense of Savannah in October 1779, the battalion remained in that town until the summer of 1780, when it marched to Ninety Six, South Carolina, via Augusta. Once there, they took part in actions at Musgrove's Mills, the relief of Augusta and Long Canes. In 1781 they contributed significantly to the defense of Ninety Six. The battalion returned to New York upon the evacuation of Charleston, and then disbanded along the Saint John River on October 10, 1783.

2nd Battalion, DeLancey's Brigade

This battalion was led by Col. George Brewerton of New York City, until his death in September 1779. The corps served primarily at Kingsbridge, New York through 1778, providing 22 men under Lt. Justin McCartney to the initial formation of Emmerick's Chasseurs. Joined 1st DeLancey's on the expedition to Georgia and had a similar history until 1780. They remained part of the garrison of Savannah until its evacuation in July 1782. Drafted into the 1st Battalion, DeLancey's on February 24, 1782.

3rd Battalion, DeLancey's Brigade

Ultimately the largest of the battalions of DeLancey's Brigade. Commanded by Col. Gabriel G. Ludlow of Queens County, the battalion served on Long Island the entire war. It defended Setauket against the forces of Gen. Samuel H. Parsons on August 22, 1777, holding out in a fortified church, and contributed 19 men under Ensign William McFarland to serve in the American Volunteers. In 1780 a light infantry company was formed under Capt. Gilbert Colden Willett, which was attached to the Provincial Light Infantry. The battalion's lieutenant colonel, Richard Hewlett, was the senior Provincial officer leading the fleet destined for the Saint John River, where the battalion was disbanded on 10 October 1783. Some members of the corps perished en route in the wreck of the *Martha* Transport.

Detroit Militia

One battalion of six companies, under the command of Maj. Jehu Hay. In 1782, the battalion mustered about 490 officers and men.

Detroit Volunteers

An embodied volunteer company (i.e., a company that remained in continual service, as opposed to most militia units, that only served when called up, for example, during an emergency) raised by Capt. Guillaume La Motte. Forty five officers and men of the company joined the garrison of Vincennes (in what would become Indiana) in December 1778. The Volunteers fought at the fall of the fort to Col. George Rogers Clark's force in February 1779, which essentially ended British power in the region. La Motte and his lieutenant, Jacob Schieffelin, were captured, but regained their freedom by 1781. Though there are few or no records of further actions by Volunteers, there are numerous references to members of the unit receiving land after the war.

Duke of Cumberland's Regiment
also known as Lord Montagu's Corps

Raised in February 1781 by Lt. Col. Lord Charles Greville Montagu, former Royal Governor of South Carolina and then captain in the British 88th Regiment of Foot. Montagu's initial recruits were enlisted from amongst Continental prisoners at Charleston, primarily those taken during the siege of Charleston and Camden. After the success in recruiting, a second battalion was formed by the amalgamation of the Loyal American Rangers, Jamaica Corps, and Jamaica Independent Company. The 2nd Battalion was commanded by Maj. John McDonald. More than 1,000 officers and men served in the two battalions. The corps had an excellent reputation for discipline and included a "band of music"—a military band. The battalions were disbanded between August and October 1783, with the men having the choice of disbandment in Jamaica, England, or Nova Scotia. The bulk of the corps settled in Manchester Township, Nova Scotia.

Dunlop's Corps

This mounted infantry and cavalry unit was based at Ninety Six, South Carolina, in December 1780. Capt. James Dunlop of the Queen's Rangers, a veteran of the battle of Brandywine and Ranger raids in New York and New Jersey, was given the rank of major and command of what then became known as Dunlop's Corps. Dunlop had been in South Carolina as a captain in Patrick Ferguson's American Volunteers. Twice wounded in South Carolina battles, in March 1781 Dunlop was wounded again and captured when his 180-man corps was defeated in a skirmish at Beattie's Mill. Fellow Provincial officers testified that he was shot to death while being held prisoner. His unit was disbanded in July 1781.

Emmerick's Chasseurs

Capt. Andreas Emmerick, a German officer serving with British forces, organized the Chasseurs in August 1777. He selected 100 active "marksmen" to be drawn from Provincial units at Kingsbridge, New York, along with 50 men probably used for bayonet support. The corps took part in Sir Henry Clinton's September 1777 New Jersey forage and shortly thereafter at the storming of Fort Montgomery and burning of Kingston. In April 1778 the corps was expanded and organized as two troops of light dragoons, one light infantry company, one rifle company, and three chasseur companies. The corps was marked by discipline problems, notably a schism between the American-born officers against Emmerick and the European-born officers. The unit was drafted on August 31, 1779, with the men primarily going to the Queen's American Rangers, Volunteers of Ireland, British Legion, New York Volunteers and the 3rd Battalion of DeLancey's Brigade. In 1809, back in Germany, Emmerick joined an insurrection against Napoleon's occupation of Hesse-Kassel. At the age of 72 he was executed by a firing squad.

Ethiopian Regiment

John Murray, Earl of Dunmore, last royal governor of Virginia, created this unit of ex-slaves. In November 1775 Dunmore issued a proclamation promising freedom to slaves who took up arms for the British. Several hundred slaves fled their masters and accepted his offer. From them he formed a regiment of several hundred men, commanded by white officers. After Dunmore's defeat at Great Bridge, Virginia, in December 1775, the regiment was involved in the evacuation of Norfolk and served British forces in the Chesapeake area. Diminished by smallpox and other diseases, the regiment sailed to British-occupied New York and was officially disbanded. However, many survivors remained in British service. They were among the more than

3,000 former slaves who migrated to Nova Scotia after the war. The commander of the regiment, Maj. Thomas Taylor Byrd, was the brother of a Rebel, Francis Byrd.

Florida Loyalist Military Units

Florida has been called the "14th colony," and the only future state that did not declare independence from Britain. In the 1763 treaty ending the French and Indian War, Britain received the Spanish colony of Florida and part of the French colony of Louisiana. The British made the new acquisition into two colonies: East Florida, with St. Augustine its capital and consisting of most of present-day Florida; and West Florida on the north shore of the Gulf of Mexico with its capital Pensacola. West Florida was bounded by the Mississippi River and Lake Pontchartrain in the west by the 31st parallel on the north and the Apalachicola River on the east. Loyalists fought Spanish rule in both colonies.

East Florida Militia

Authorized in August 1776 by Governor Patrick Tonyn, eleven companies of militia were formed into one regiment, commanded by Col. John Moultrie. In 1779, a second regiment was formed, commanded by Lt. Col. Henry Yonge. The militia included both black and white inhabitants. A company of men was formed from Minorcans at the New Smyrna settlement. The militia was greatly expanded, at least on paper, after the influx of refugees from the evacuations of Savannah and Charleston.

East Florida Militia Light Horse

Commanded by Lt. Col. William Young of South Carolina, these troops served in 1783 to protect the inhabitants and refugees from attack by outlaws on the borders.

East Florida Rangers
(see also King's Carolina Rangers)

Authorized in June 1776 by Governor Patrick Tonyn, this local corps was raised and commanded by Lt. Col. Thomas Brown, a recent emigrant from the Orkney Islands to Georgia. Recruited primarily from Georgia refugees, the corps consisted of four, and later six, mounted troops. Brown's corps made frequent excursions into Georgia and was a part of Gen. Augustine Prevost's invasion in January 1779. No longer serving in East Florida, whose colonial government was paying the bills of the corps, it was disbanded on June 30, 1779 and reformed the next day as a Provincial regiment, the King's (Carolina) Rangers, a foot regiment with the same officer structure.

East Florida Volunteers

Raised in East Florida by Capt. Henry Yonge in 1777, this local independent company was likewise a part of Prevost's invasion of Georgia in January 1779. Unlike the Rangers, it soon after returned to St. Augustine, where it was disbanded the following year.

Natchez Volunteers

Raised by Maj. John Blommart on April 22, 1781, this volunteer corps consisted of six companies of infantry, one of artillery, and a troop of horse. Blommart led what came to be known as the "Natchez Rebellion" against the Spanish, leading to the capture of Fort Panmure. The capture of Pensacola by the Spanish the following May led to the end of British support to the remaining subjects in West Florida and the frontier beyond. Blommart and a handful of others were imprisoned in New Orleans, while the remainder of the corps was disbanded on June 22, 1781. Blommart and the others were not released until October 1783.

West Florida Independent Provincial Company

Raised by Capt. Francis Miller in 1778, this small unit was raised under the auspices of West Florida's colonial government. Miller and the bulk of the company were captured at Baton Rouge in September 1779.

West Florida Independent Rangers

Raised by Capt. Thaddeus Lyman in 1778, by order of Governor Peter Chester, in response to James Willings' raid down the Mississippi. The company continued in service through the surrender of Pensacola in May 1781, when it surrendered as part of the garrison. After the surrender, Capt. Lyman, along with his brothers Oliver and Thompson of the same company, retired to the Mississippi where they fetched their families and made their way overland through Indian country to the British garrison of Savannah, Georgia.

West Florida Loyal Refugees

This corps, raised under the authority of John Stuart of the Indian Department, originally consisted of two mounted troops, later expanding to four. The troops acted independently, working with the native tribes and patrolling along the coast and the Mississippi.

West Florida Militia

West Florida was without a militia law, but in 1779 volunteer companies were encouraged by Governor Peter Chester. One such was commanded by Capt. Patrick Strachen, who later commanded a troop in the West Florida Royal Foresters.

West Florida Provincials

Under the command of Lt. Col. John McGillivray, this corps was raised on March 18, 1778 by order of Governor Peter Chester and the government of West Florida. With only 96 officers and men, and a strain on the finances of the province, the corps was disbanded later the same year. Lt. Col. McGillivray was captured at sea en route to Savannah, Georgia, by a squadron of Spanish ships. He was held prisoner at Havana for the remainder of the war.

West Florida Royal Foresters

Authorized as a three-troop corps on February 5, 1780, this was the only Provincial unit raised in the Province of West Florida. Each troop acted independently, with Capt. Adam Chrystie as senior officer to the whole. At the siege of Mobile in March 1780 Capt. Charles Walker was killed and his troop surrendered with the garrison. A second troop, under Capt. Patrick Strachan, was taken prisoner shortly thereafter. Capt. Chrystie's troop took part in the unsuccessful assault on Mobile Village in January 1781 and in the Provincial sortie from the works at Pensacola five months later. Capt. Chrystie and the survivors of the troop surrendered with the garrison and spent the following year at New York as prisoners on parole to Spain. The troop appears to have been disbanded shortly after their exchange in 1782.

West Florida Volunteers

An independent militia company raised in 1780 and commanded by Capt. Hubert Rees. Its history appears to have been short-lived.

Forshner's Independent Company

Authorized at New York City in August 1780 as an independent Provincial company under the command of Capt. Andrew Forshner, only twenty men were ever enlisted in this corps. Forshner himself appears to have been used to gather intelligence, occasionally with his men. Most of the remaining soldiers still serving in August 1781 were drafted into the King's American Regiment and the British Legion.

Garrison Battalion
also known as Royal Garrison Battalion

The unit was formed in New York City in October 1778 under the command of Maj. William Sutherland of the British Army and sent to Bermuda to defend against a French or American attack that never happened. The British feared that pro-American Bermudians would aid invaders. (Sutherland earlier had been commander of the Caledonian Volunteers.) Detachments of the Garrison Battalion served at New York, Halifax and Charlestown. When Paulus Hook was attacked by Continentals under Maj. Henry Lee, the defending force consisted of men of the Garrison Battalion under Maj. Sutherland. Two companies were captured in May 1782 at New Providence. The corps was formed predominantly of British soldiers who were invalids or worn out in the service, but still capable of limited duty. On December 25, 1782 the corps was made a regular regiment of the British Army. The regiment was disbanded by companies between June and October 1783.

Georgia Loyalist Military Units

Georgia, the only colony to be restored to its British civil government during the Revolution, fostered several Loyalist military units with many British and American commanders.

Georgia Artillery

Raised in Savannah by Capt. William Wylly in 1781 and later commanded by Capt. Alexander McGoun. He had been named by the Rebels' Council of Safety in Georgia as a person "whose going at large is dangerous to the liberties of America." The Rebels later confiscated his property, along with the property of 224 others named by the Council. The company was a part of the Georgia Militia establishment and served until the evacuation of Savannah in 1782.

Georgia Light Dragoons

The first Provincial unit raised after the taking of Savannah in December 1778. Initially two troops, commanded by Captains Archibald Campbell and Thomas Tawse, officers in the 71st Highlanders. The troops were created by drafts from the 71st, New York Volunteers and DeLancey's Brigade, as well as recruits raised in Georgia. The troops served at Briar Creek, Stono Ferry, and the siege of Savannah, where Capt. Tawse was killed. After the siege, the two troops were combined to one under Capt. Campbell and were attached to the British Legion for the 1780 Campaign in South Carolina. It appears to have been disbanded around June 1781.

Georgia Light Dragoons (Militia)

After months of unsuccessfully soliciting cavalry units from Lord Cornwallis, Governor Sir James Wright and the Georgia Assembly in late 1780 authorized two uniformed troops of cavalry be raised at the expense of the province. Commanded by Captains Henry Ferguson and John Lightenstone, these troops acted independently of the two troops of Provincial cavalry in the province. The troops were disbanded on the evacuation of the province in July 1782.

Georgia Loyalists

Raised in Georgia in May 1779 by Maj. James Wright, Jr., son to Georgia's royal governor. Initially six companies of infantry, the corps was reduced to three companies in 1780. It did garrison duty at Savannah for most of its existence, taking part in the siege there in 1779. The three companies, consisting of about 150 men, were made a part of the King's (Carolina) Rangers on February 24, 1782.

Georgia Militia

One of the first tasks initiated after the taking of Savannah by Lt. Col. Archibald Campbell's expedition was the raising of Loyalist militia. This became more formal upon the reinstatement of Royal Governor Sir James Wright and the Georgia Assembly. Five regiments of infantry were raised in the different districts of the province, from which horse patrols were created. A rifle company under Capt. Benjamin Brantley was also raised. Detachments of the militia were involved in numerous skirmishes throughout the frontier. The 2nd Regiment, under Col. James Grierson, took part in the fighting that led to the loss of Augusta in June 1781. Grierson himself was shot and killed while a prisoner. The militia was disbanded in 1782 on the evacuation of the province.

Georgia Rangers

This mounted corps was authorized in 1773 by Governor James Wright of Georgia. Commanded by Capt. Edward Bernard until his death in 1775, the unit was to patrol the "Ceded Lands" in the west of the province. The unit served until the revolution overturned the government in 1776. Many of the officers and men later found their way into the militia or Provincial units.

Georgia Rifle Dragoons

Raised in January 1779, by Maj. Thomas Fleming. Fleming was captured soon afterwards, and it is unlikely the corps continued without him.

Royal Georgia Volunteers

The first new Provincial infantry unit authorized after the conquest of Savannah. Raised by Maj. Dougald Campbell in January 1779, the corps only raised about 25 men, who were mostly incorporated a few months later into the New York Volunteers.

Volunteers of Augusta

A volunteer militia cavalry corps of two or three troops, raised on the establishment of the Georgia Militia. The corps consisted of refugees from Augusta after the loss of that city and took part in several skirmishes in 1782 near Savannah.

Golding's Company of Volunteers

Raised by Capt. Joseph Golding or Golden in 1776, this Provincial New York company was probably merged into the Queen's American Rangers the following year.

Governor Wentworth's Volunteers

A troop of cavalry organized in 1777 on Long Island under the command of Capt. Daniel Murray. Named in honor of Royal Governor John Wentworth of New Hampshire, the troop consisted primarily of prominent New England Loyalists. Stationed on Long Island throughout its existence, it took part in several expeditions in 1779 in conjunction with the Loyal Associated Refugees out of Rhode Island. Many of its members would go on to become officers in other Provincial units, primarily the King's American Dragoons. The troop was disbanded in 1781.

Grenada Militia

In 1779, the militia of this island consisted of at least four infantry regiments, as well as one of horse. With the French capture of Grenada on July 4, 1779, the militia's service for the British ceased.

Guides and Pioneers

This corps was raised in 1776, probably the brainchild of Maj. Samuel Holland, the unit's second commander. During the 1776 Campaign, Capt. Andreas Emmerick was in command. Pioneers performed the support duties of felling trees, clearing obstructions and facilitating assaults on fortifications. The unit was unique in that it initially served under terms of a one-year engagement. The corps in effect disbanded in Philadelphia in December 1777 and was reformed immediately thereafter under the normal terms of enlistment for Provincial forces, i.e. the duration of the war. The corps was raised primarily from Loyalists in Connecticut, New York, New Jersey and Pennsylvania. After a succession of commanders, the unit was led by Maj. John Aldington, a brewer from Bergen County, New Jersey. Primarily in detachments, the unit fought at Danbury, the Philadelphia Campaign, Monmouth, the relief of Newport, the 1778 Grand Forage, the siege of

Charleston, Camden, the expeditions to Virginia under Generals Leslie, Arnold and Phillips. The corps was disbanded on October 10, 1783 along the Saint John River.

Guides and Pioneers (Southern)

Three companies of armed and unarmed blacks were raised during the siege of Savannah, under the command of Maj. Daniel Manson, a captain of the Royal North Carolina Regiment. The corps afterwards served at the siege of Charleston and remained there until the evacuation of that city in December 1782. Some were then sent to New York, where they joined the Black Pioneers, while others helped form the new Black Carolina Corps.

Harkimer's Bateau Company

Bateaux were mid-sized boats used for various tasks. Capt. Jost Harkimer raised an independent company of bateau-men in Canada in the summer of 1780, which corps served until it was disbanded on December 24, 1783. Harkimer had previously served in the Indian Department and also in charge of the bateaux during the expedition against Fort Stanwix by Lt. Col. Barry St. Leger in August 1777.

Hatfield's Company of Partisans

Commanded by Capt. Cornelius Hatfield or Hetfield, Jr., this company of "active young volunteers" captured as many as 300 enemy militia and Continental troops in New Jersey, opposite Staten Island. The company also operated armed boats in the kills around the island. Hatfield, an inhabitant of Elizabethtown, New Jersey, raided his hometown on numerous occasions.

Hazard's Corps of Refugees

In the fall of 1780, Capt. Thomas Hazard (or Haszard) of Rhode Island was authorized to raise a company of 100 men on Long Island. On November 23, 1780, over half the corps was killed or captured at St. George's Manor, Long Island. The unit apparently disbanded in 1782.

Hewetson's Corps

James Hewetson, a retired British Army ensign, received a warrant to raise a battalion of 700 men in early 1777. He was captured while recruiting, and only a few recruits drawn from Livingston Manor ever joined the British. After Hewetson was hanged at Albany on July 4, 1777, the recruits joined the army under Gen. Burgoyne.

Independent Companies
Also known as Hierlihy's Corps

Initially intended as a second battalion to the Prince of Wales' American Volunteers, this 200-man corps was raised in early 1777 by Maj. Timothy Hierlihy of Connecticut, a veteran with lengthy Provincial service in the French and Indian War. After serving their first year at New York, in which they provided support to Emmerick's Chasseurs, Hierlihy and the companies embarked for Nova Scotia and shortly thereafter for the Island of Saint John's. Hierlihy and his corps would occupy the island until 1782, when they were relieved by the 1st Battalion, King's American Rangers. Hierlihy and the companies would then proceed to Halifax, where they were merged into the Nova Scotia Volunteers, with Hierlihy as the new lieutenant colonel.

Jamaica Independent Company

Formed at Bluefields in what is now Belize from survivors of various Jamaica and Mosquito Coast units. Originally to have been two companies, but only enough to form one, commanded by Capt. John Davis. This Provincial company served during the loss of Rattan (Roatán) to the Spanish in 1782. Survivors eventually drafted into the 2nd Battalion of the Duke of Cumberland's Regiment.

Jamaica Corps
also known as Amherst's Corps

Raised at Charleston, South Carolina by Capt. Jeffrey Amherst, a captain in the 1st Battalion, 60th Regiment of Foot, for service in Jamaica. One company of about 100 men was raised in March 1781, primarily from Continental prisoners of war and drafts from the Loyal Irish Corps, a regular unit serving in Jamaica. The company, intended to raid Spanish settlements in Central America, would form a part of the garrison of Jamaica. Along with the Loyal American Rangers, the company helped form the nucleus of the 2nd Battalion, Duke of Cumberland's Regiment in 1783.

Jamaica Rangers

The idea of raising black troops in Jamaica was proposed by Governor John Dalling as early as May 1779. A battalion of blacks was raised by William Henry Ricketts and did duty on the island into early 1780. At the objection of merchants and planters residing in England however, the corps was ordered disbanded in February 1780. With the threat of French-Spanish invasion in 1782, the idea was once again revived. This time two Provincial battalions were authorized by Brigadier Gen. Archibald Campbell, commanding on the island, and once again William Henry Ricketts would step forward, as major commandant of the 1st Battalion of Jamaica Rangers; William Lewis, who had previously commanded the light dragoons, would serve as major commandant of the corps' 2nd battalion. It is unknown how many men enlisted, although 75 were recruited at New York City for the 2nd battalion in the summer of 1783. A third battalion was authorized in November 1782, to be commanded by Nathaniel Beckford. All battalions were disbanded at the end of 1783.

Jamaica Local Military Units

In 1655, the British captured Jamaica and used the plantation slavery of Jamaica to launch the triangular trade: England's manufactured goods, Africa's slaves, and the Caribbean's sugar. When Spain entered the Revolutionary War as a French ally, Britain needed to protect Jamaica.

Jamaica Legion

Raised March 1780 at Kingston, Jamaica by Col. William Dalrymple, the adjutant general of the army on the island. On inspection they were noted as "…composed chiefly of Privateer's Men (under which description were included some people of Colour) and a few Inhabitants of this Island. This corps, on being reviewed by Brigadier Genl. Campbell appeared to him a riotous troublesome set of people." There were initially 213 men raised for the Legion, of whom 150 were reported dead by the end of the year after service in Central America. The survivors were later amalgamated into the Jamaica Volunteers and then the Jamaica Independent Company.

Jamaica Light Dragoons

Raised at Kingston, Jamaica by Maj. William Lewis. Their inspection recorded their composition: "Light Horse, or Dragoons raised about the beginning of July [1780,] (notwithstanding the address of the House to the governor some months before for putting a Stop to levies in the Island) amounted to 98 but only 58 of them appear to have been sent to the main. They consisted of Curacoa men, Sailors, Italians, Portuguese, a few People of Colour belonging to the Island, and 16 or 18 white Inhabitants including Officers." The bulk of the men died in service against the Spanish in Central America; the survivors helped form the Jamaica Independent Company.

Jamaica Militia

By war's end, the Jamaica Militia was the largest force on the island, boasting eighteen battalions of militia infantry, along with three "divisions" of horse, totaling around 8,000 men, including a division of grenadiers.

Jamaica Volunteers
also known as Royal Jamaica Volunteers

Raised in Jamaica in October 1779. The unit, of about 240 men, took part in a campaign aimed at weakening Spanish power in South America. In 1780 a British amphibious force—whose ships were commanded by Capt. Horatio Nelson, the future hero of Trafalgar—landed on the coast of today's Nicaragua and ascended the San Juan River. Under the command of Maj. John McDonald, they appear to have been the best of the volunteer corps raised for the 1780 Central American expedition, even after losing 120 dead within the first few months of their landing on the Spanish Main. The survivors of the other volunteer corps were merged into the Volunteers, who in turn provided the bulk of men for the Jamaica Independent Company.

Royal Batteaux Volunteers
or Royal Batteaux Men

Raised in Jamaica in 1779 by Sir Alexander Leith for the handling of small craft along the rivers and lakes of Central America. Described by their agent, James Smith, thus: "they consisted of about 150 men at the time of their Embarkation under Sir Alexr. Leith, that they consisted mostly of Curracoa men of Colour Collected from amongst the Prisoners of War, & about Town and also of Seamen Voluntarily inlisted and this Examinant believes there were among them few natives of Colour, beside white Officers." As an under strength unit, merged into the Jamaica Volunteers.

James Island Troop of Light Dragoons
also known as James Island Troop of Horse

This small unit, 34 officers and men in number, was raised on James Island, South Carolina by Capt. Alexander Stewart in June of 1781. Stewart was a Loyalist from South Carolina who had joined the British during the siege of Charleston in 1780, after having been wounded in the attempt the previous year. The troop was raised by order of Col. Balfour, commandant of Charleston, but appears to have been mustered as a Provincial unit, later considered as militia.

King's American Dragoons

One of the last but most successful Provincial units to be raised during the war. The brainchild of Timothy Ruggles and Daniel Murray of Massachusetts, the corps was proposed in 1780 and authorized early the following year. The command was given to Lt. Col. Benjamin Thompson of New Hampshire, then serving as Undersecretary of State for American Affairs, under Lord George Germain. The unit was formed at New York City initially by drafts from the Loyal New Englanders and Stewart's Light Dragoons, with a number of officers elevated from the ranks of Wentworth's Volunteers. The corps fought in no battles, but had the honor of having its colors presented by Prince William Henry at Brooklyn in 1782. Lt. Col. Thompson, along with several recruits he brought out from England, served briefly but with distinction at Charleston in January and February 1782 before joining the corps at New York City. The unit became the first Provincial regiment sent to the Saint John River in the summer of 1783, where they were disbanded on October 10 of that year. Lt. Col. Thompson would later follow scientific pursuits, becoming Count Rumford, who deduced that heat was not a fluid.

Benjamin Thompson,
Count Rumford

King's American Rangers

On May 1 1779, Lt. Col. Robert Rogers, the disgraced former commander of the Queen's American Rangers, received a warrant to raise a corps of rangers, consisting of two battalions, each of a thousand men. Rogers turned to seconded officers of other corps, including his brother James (formerly of the Royal American Reformees) to raise the men. James Rogers led a number of these officers and some volunteers to Quebec, where they raised three companies. This would become the 2nd battalion of the corps. Robert Rogers, sending highly unrealistic reports to England and incurring huge debts for which he was

Robert Rogers
mezzotint by Thomas Hart, 1776
Fort Ticonderoga Museum

unable to repay, eventually ended up in prison before removing to England. Those remaining at New York City would end up under the command of Capt. Samuel Hayden, formerly of the New Jersey Volunteers. These men would become the 1st battalion of the corps, serving from 1781 to 1783 in Nova Scotia and the Island of Saint John's (Prince Edward Island). Neither battalion fought in any major action and both were disbanded at the end of 1783.

King's American Regiment
also known as the 4th American Regiment

Raised on Long Island, New York, this regiment of ten companies was one of the best of the Provincial units, recruiting over 900 men. Members came from the Hudson River Valley, New York City, Connecticut, and Rhode Island. The corps fought in Rhode Island in 1778, in Connecticut in 1779, in the expedition to Virginia under Gen. Alexander Leslie in 1780, at Hobkirk's Hill, South Carolina in 1781, and in skirmishes outside Savannah in 1782. The commander, Col. Edmund Fanning, was secretary to William Tryon, royal governor successively of North Carolina and New York. When Maj. Gen. Tryon raided New Haven, Fanning, a graduate of Yale, intervened to save his alma mater from being destroyed. In gratitude, Yale in 1803 awarded him an honorary doctorate. The light infantry company of the battalion, under Capt. Thomas Cornwell, became a part of the Provincial Light Infantry in August 1780. A detachment of men under Capt. Abraham DePeyster became a part of Patrick Ferguson's American Volunteers in December 1779. A troop of light dragoons under Capt. Isaac Atwood was added in June 1781, shortly after the unit's arrival at Savannah. The regiment was made the 4th American Regiment in 1781, and then put on the British Establishment as a regular regiment on December 25, 1782. It was disbanded on the Saint John River on 10 October 1783.

Edmund Fanning
New York Public Library

King's Carolina Rangers
also known as King's Florida Rangers and King's Rangers

This famous Provincial corps was created in June 1779, based
on the old East Florida Rangers, both of which units were
commanded by Lt. Col. Thomas Brown. After taking part in the
successful defense of Savannah in 1779, the corps was sent to
establish a post at Augusta, Georgia. It won renown for its defense
of that place against a large force under Col. Elijah Clarke in
September of 1780. A second engagement at that place, led by
Lt. Col. Henry Lee, ended in the surrender of Lt. Col. Brown and
the corps on June 5, 1781. After a general exchange in the South,
Brown and the corps quickly returned to active service outside

of Savannah. A troop of cavalry was raised out of the corps in the fall of 1781, commanded by Capt. Alexander Campbell Wylly. The corps fought in several actions in the spring of 1782 against Continental troops under Gen. Anthony Wayne. At the evacuation of Savannah, the corps was sent to Charleston, where it remained until sent to St. Augustine in October 1782. The corps served here until sent to Nova Scotia towards the end of 1783, where it was disbanded.

King's Loyal Americans

The first of what would become known as the "Royalist" corps, ninety men under Lt. Col. Ebenezer Jessup joined the army under Sir Guy Carleton on November 4, 1776. The bulk of the corps would be raised the following year during the Burgoyne Campaign, reaching a strength of seven companies and 337 officers and men. Losing many men taken in skirmishes and scouts, along with deaths, desertions, detachment and transfers to McAlpin's Corps, just 115 remained after the battle of Saratoga. The remains became a part of the Convention of Saratoga. With the convention nullified in the summer of 1778, the remains of the corps existed for the next few years doing duty mostly in detachment form, serving as marines, working on fortifications, and other similar duties. In November 1781, the King's Loyal Americans, along with the other Royalist units, were merged together to form the Provincial corps of Loyal Rangers, commanded by Ebenezer's brother, Maj. Edward Jessup.

King's Militia Volunteers

Devised in February 1779 by Governor William Franklin of New Jersey, this corps was a loose association of independent refugee companies serving principally at Bergen Point, Sandy Hook, and Long Island. The companies operated independently, and without the pay, uniforms, provisions, etc. given to Provincial

Forces. Their greatest military success came on May 1, 1779 when a small detachment in whaleboats captured Brigadier Gen. Gold Selleck Silliman in Fairfield, Connecticut and safely returned him to Long Island.

King's Orange Rangers

Authorized on Christmas Day, 1776, this Provincial regiment was commanded by Lt. Col. John Bayard, a lieutenant in the British 60th Regiment of Foot. Bayard was the son of William Bayard, prominent land owner in Bergen County, New Jersey and Orange County New York, in which latter place William was colonel of the militia. The corps took part in Sir Henry Clinton's 1777 New Jersey Grand Forage and his Hudson River expedition. The corps fell into turmoil when Lt. Col. Bayard was put under arrest for murdering one of his lieutenants, William Bird, on March 10, 1778. Without its commander, numerous desertions followed over the course of the summer, leading to the unit's being transferred to Halifax, Nova Scotia in October 1778. There, and by detachment to Liverpool, the corps remained until the end of the war. Numerous recruits were raised in Newfoundland, starting in 1779. A party of these Newfoundland recruits was blown to England on their voyage to Nova Scotia, not joining the corps for almost two years, via New York City. The corps was disbanded in Nova Scotia on October 10, 1783.

King's Royal Regiment of New York

The regiment was raised by Lt. Col. Sir John Johnson, son of the foremost British Indian agent in North America, Sir William Johnson. The corps was formed on June 19, 1776, after Sir John led over two hundred of his tenants from the area of Johnson Hall in the Mohawk Valley to Montreal. The regiment served in Lt. Col. Barry St. Leger's 1777 campaign against Fort Stanwix. Sir John and the light infantry company of the regiment fought at the famous battle of Oriskany. While the expedition failed, it did have the affect of adding two new companies and a hundred new recruits to the corps. The corps, as a whole or in detachment

Lt. Col. Sir John Johnson
Library and Archives Canada

form, served annually in raids into New York, particularly the Mohawk Valley, some led by Sir John himself. A second battalion was added in 1780, commanded by Maj. John Ross, who commanded his own raid into the Mohawk Valley in October 1781. The battalions were disbanded separately, the 1st at Montreal on 24 December 1783 and the 2nd on June 24, 1784. Both battalions were instrumental in forming the new province of Upper Canada, now Ontario.

Kinloch's Light Dragoons

One of the first Provincial cavalry units to be raised, this independent troop was raised at New York by Capt. David Kinloch, an officer from the 71st Highlanders. The troop served at New York and on Long Island until it was made a part of the British Legion on August 1, 1778.

Locke's Independent Company

Joshua Locke, a veteran Ranger officer from the French and Indian War, received a warrant at New York in June 1779 to raise an independent Provincial Company. The effort was unsuccessful and the few recruits raised were drafted into other corps.

Loyal American Association

Amongst the very first Loyalist units of the war, the Association took the place of Boston's militia during the siege. In response to a request of the principal inhabitants of Boston, the unit was commissioned on July 5, 1775 and divided into five companies, under the command of its senior captain, Timothy Ruggles. A 64-year-old native of America when the war broke out, Ruggles had served as colonel of the Massachusetts Provincial Regiment and a brigadier general during the French and Indian War. The corps' primary duty was to assist in the internal security of the town, looking out for "Fires, Thieves, Rob[b]ers, house breakers or Rioters." The corps was reorganized into three companies in November 1775 by Gen. William Howe on his taking over command of the army. The corps was disbanded on the evacuation of the city the following March.

Loyal American Rangers

Looking to add strength to the garrison of Jamaica, and provide a new means for raiding the Spanish Main, Maj. William Odell of the Jamaica Militia was dispatched to New York City, seeking to raise a corps primarily from prisoners of war. Sir Henry Clinton acquiesced, limiting the prisoners, however, to those in the naval line. Odell recruited tirelessly, in person or through recruiting officers, at New York, Charleston, Wilmington, and Savannah, raising no less than 475 men, divided into six companies. The corps was dispatched from Jamaica for the relief of Pensacola in March 1781, although their ships turned back before reaching that place. The corps served the remainder of 1781 and 1782 either in Jamaica or by detachments in Honduras and at the loss of the Island of Rattan. After the death of Lt. Col. Odell and the corps' major, Alexander Campbell, it was decided to incorporate the Rangers with the Jamaica Corps, forming the 2nd Battalion, Duke of Cumberland's Regiment on January 25, 1783.

Loyal American Regiment

Raised by Col. Beverley Robinson in the Hudson Valley of New York in March 1777. Robinson was a very wealthy land owner in Dutchess County, New York, near West Point, but formerly of Virginia. His son, Beverley Robinson, Jr. eventually became his second in command, and his son-in-law, Thomas Barclay, the major. Other sons and relations likewise became officers, including a very young Frederick Philipse Robinson, who would later be knighted and attain the rank of major general while serving in the War of 1812. The Loyal Americans would eventually enlist more than 840 men, fighting at the storming of Fort Montgomery in 1777, Horseneck, Verplanck, and Stony Point in 1779, Hopperstown in 1780, Virginia, Pleasant Valley, and finally New London in 1781. Their light infantry company under Capt. Morris Robinson became a part of the Provincial Light Infantry in August 1780. An additional detachment

All GENTLEMEN VOLUNTEERS,
Who are wil'ing to ferve his Majefty in the
LOYAL AMERICAN REGIMENT
COMMANDED BY
Col. BEVERLEY ROBINSON,
Eor TWO YEARS, or during the Rebel-
lion, fhall upon their being muftered and ap-
proved of by the Infpector-General, receive
Twenty-five Dollars Bounty.
Whatever Perfons are willing to embrace the
prefent Opportunity offered or approving their
Loyalty, let them repair to the Quarters of the
Regiment, at Haerlem Heights, or to the
Bull's Head Tavern, at New-York, where an
Officer will attend to receive and entertain them.

Recruiting Notice for the Loyal American Regiment

served under Lt. Duncan Fletcher under Patrick Ferguson in the American Volunteers. The corps was disbanded along the Saint John River on October 10, 1783.

Loyal Associated Refugees

Organized in early 1779 by George Leonard, a Massachusetts Loyalist, the unit was a sea-going raiding force of Loyalist sailors and soldiers operating out of Newport, Rhode Island. The military wing of the corps was commanded by Col. Edmund Fanning of the King's American Regiment, seconded by Lt. Col. Edward Winslow, the muster master general of provincial forces. The naval force of about 400 sailors operated five major ships: the Frigate *Restoration*, the Sloop *General Prescott*, and the schooners *Charlotte, General Leslie,* and *General Garth*, besides five other armed schooners and transports. The principal warships were issued letters of marquee and retaliation as privateers, enabling them to make prizes of enemy shipping. The members of the corps as Leonard described them, were "of a rank in life superior to the class from which the common seaman and soldier are taken, they were averse to entering into the service, as such, and still more to remaining idle spectators of the contest." With the evacuation of Rhode Island in October 1779 the corps was put of business, although its framework contributed greatly to the formation of the Associated Loyalists later on in the war.

Loyal Foresters

Authorized by Sir Henry Clinton at New York City around April, 1781, this Provincial unit was commanded by Lt. Col. John Connolly, the Virginian who had just spent five years as a prisoner to the Congressional forces for his failed attempt to raise the Queen's Royal Rangers for Lord Dunmore. Connolly and a few recruits joined Lord Cornwallis' Army in Virginia in June 1781, seeking to complete the corps. The lieutenant colonel was made prisoner during the siege of Yorktown by inadvertently straying outside the lines. Many of the remaining men in the corps later were among the troops surrendered by Cornwallis on October 19, 1781. The remainder of the corps was organized into one company, commanded by Capt. Alexander McDonald of Philadelphia, formerly a lieutenant in the Guides and Pioneers. The corps was made the 10th company of the 1st Battalion, New Jersey Volunteers on April 8, 1782. See entry for *Queen's Loyal Rangers.*

Loyal Irish Volunteers

A number of Irish inhabitants of Boston, most of who were probably already doing duty in the Loyal American Association, petitioned Gen. William Howe for permission to form their own company, which was granted on December 7, 1775. The company was commanded by Capt. James Forrest, a long-established merchant of Boston. The company did the same general duties as the Loyal American Association and was likewise disbanded on the evacuation of the town in 1776. Capt. Forrest would be captured at sea that same year and suffer a lengthy imprisonment in Philadelphia.

Loyal New Englanders

Authorized by Sir William Howe on March 21, 1777, this Provincial unit was raised by Lt. Col. George Wightman, a fifty-year-old Rhode Island farmer. Even after the corps absorbed the drafts from the Loyal Rhode Islanders, only three companies were raised. The corps took part in the 1778 siege of Newport. Detachments of the corps occasionally took part in 1779 raids with the Loyal Associated Refugees. On the evacuation of Newport, the corps removed to Lloyd's Neck, the principal British fortification on the north shore of Long Island. Here they remained until drafted as an under-strength corps on or about June 9, 1781. The drafted men primarily entered the King's American Dragoons.

Loyal Newport Associators

Authorized by Maj. Gen. Robert Pigot on October 15, 1777 "for the Purpose of preserving the internal Peace and Security of the Town," this four company corps was commanded by Col. Joseph Wanton, a former Rhode Island militia officer and deputy governor. About one hundred and eighty men initially did duty when Rhode Island was threatened with invasion by militia from the main in October 1777. The corps was disbanded shortly before the evacuation of Rhode Island in October 1779.

Loyal Rangers

The last Provincial unit raised in the Northern Army, this corps was commissioned on November 25, 1781 and commanded by Maj. Edward Jessup. Formed by the amalgamation of the four Royalist corps (Queen's Loyal Rangers, King's Loyal Americans, McAlpin's and Leake's) and a new company formed by Capt. John Walden Meyer. About 600 men, formed into nine companies, finally brought order and stability into the units raised years earlier during the Burgoyne Campaign. Fought in no major battles but participated in different scouts along the southern border of Quebec. The corps was disbanded on 24 December 1783.

Loyal Refugee Volunteers

Authorized in October 1779 as a corps of woodcutters by warrant from Sir Henry Clinton, the unit was raised by Abraham C. Cuyler, the former mayor of Albany, New York. This unit was unique in that it operated as a for-profit military organization, receiving no pay, arms, uniforms or provisions from the British, but would receive money for firewood, in an exclusive contract with the Barrack Master General's Department, and wood cut for fortifications. That money would be supplemented by the proceeds from cattle and plunder obtained by raids into the countryside. The military composition of the unit initially consisted of four companies of infantry, one of artillery, and a troop of horse, commanded by Capt. Thomas Ward, a deserter from Washington's Army who had served as sergeant in Malcolm's Additional Regiment. The corps established its first post at Bull's Ferry, New Jersey, where they defeated a force of a thousand Pennsylvania Continentals under Gen. Anthony Wayne on July 21, 1780. Business mistrust between Cuyler and Ward led to a schism in the corps, some following Cuyler out to Smithtown, Long Island to establish a new post, others with Ward to set up post at Bergen Point, New Jersey. Ward's part of the corps would prove much more successful, expanding to about 350 men in eight companies, including one of riflemen. The group on Long Island would be commanded by Maj. Philip Van Alstine. Both sections would be disbanded in 1782, those under Ward becoming the first Loyalists to immigrate to Nova Scotia.

Loyal Rhode Islanders
Raised in Newport in March 1777 under Col. Edward Cole, a veteran of the French and Indian War, the unit was drafted as an under-strength corps in November 1777. The two dozen or so recruits raised were drafted at that point into the Loyal New Englanders.

Maryland Loyalists
The most successful of the Provincial infantry units raised at Philadelphia after that city fell to the British. The unit was commanded by Lt. Col. James Chalmers, serving by commission from Sir William Howe, dated October 14, 1777. More than 500 officers and men served in the corps. In October 1778 the unit was sent from New York to Pensacola, West Florida, briefly stopping first at Jamaica. Smallpox ravaged the unit in early 1779, after their arrival in West Florida. Due to these high losses, and similar deaths among the Pennsylvania Loyalists,

the garrison commander, Gen. John Campbell, combined the two into the "United Corps of Pennsylvania and Maryland Loyalists." Sir Henry Clinton restored the two corps to unique identities by the beginning of 1781. The corps surrendered to the Spanish as part of the capitulation of Pensacola in May 1781. After their exchange the following year, the survivors did garrison duty on Long Island. They were disbanded on the Saint John River on October 10, 1783, although a number were lost shortly beforehand on the loss of the *Martha* transport, wrecked on the rocks of the Tusket River, near the Bay of Fundy.

Maryland Royal Retaliators

Nearly 1,300 Loyalists swore oaths to join this corps, raised by Marylanders Hugh Kelly and James Fleming, mainly in Pennsylvania. The Retaliators had ambitious plans to recruit as many as 4,000 men for a campaign to aid the British in the taking of a large swath of Pennsylvania and Maryland. But Rebels learned of the plan, arrested Kelly and some 170 men; three were convicted of treason against Maryland and hanged. Fleming and others escaped to join British forces in North Carolina. After the British surrender at Yorktown, both men made their way to British-occupied New York. Kelly was later reported living in Nova Scotia.

McAlpin's Corps of Royalists

In 1774 Daniel McAlpin, a retired officer in the 60th Regiment of Foot, bought about 1,000 acres on the west side of Saratoga Lake and became a prosperous farmer. After Rebels seized his property, he became a soldier again. In 1777, he received a warrant from Gen. Sir William Howe to raise a corps. Although authorized by Howe as a part of the Army in America, McAlpin's Corps became a part of the Northern Army, joining the troops advancing south under Burgoyne. At least 210 officers and men were raised during the campaign, only 38 of whom escaped capture. or becoming a part of the Convention of Saratoga. After the return of those who had been under convention, the corps was mostly assigned to garrison duty and fortification construction in Quebec Province. Although seriously ill, McAlpin continued in command until he died in July 1780. The 130 men left in the corps became a part of the Loyal Rangers on their formation, November 25, 1781.

Nassau Blues

Raised in 1779 by the commander of the King's County, New York Militia, Col. William Axtell. This Provincial unit was to have been raised by drafting 500 militia from the counties of King's, Queens and Suffolk for duty in Brooklyn during the course of one campaign, then be discharged. The name Nassau refers to Long Island, home of the three counties. Resistance to the plan from the militia commanders scrapped that part of the scheme, and only 63 officers and men were raised. Before the corps was disbanded on December 31, 1779, eight men under Capt. Lt. Frederick DePeyster became a part of Patrick Ferguson's American Volunteers. DePeyster and the survivors of this detachment would later become a part of the New York Volunteers. (Note: the term *Captain Lieutenant* refers to the regiment's senior lieutenant, who commanded the colonel's company.)

Negroe Volunteers

This unit was raised in Savannah during the 1779 siege of that British-held city by a joint American-French force. Unlike ex-slaves given menial Army chores elsewhere, the Negroe Volunteers were used as soldiers armed to fight the besiegers. One of the two armed companies was commanded by Capt. Hartwel Pantecost (who would later become an officer in the James Island Light Dragoons); the other by Capt. John McKenzie of the British Legion. The unit was probably disbanded by the end of the year.

Newfoundland Regiment

Raised in September 1780 as a Provincial unit at St. John's, Newfoundland by Maj. Robert Pringle. The unit was distinctive in its blue coats faced with red. Originally organized into six companies, in 1782 it was reorganized into only three, but with the same number of officers and men, about 350. On December 25, 1782 it was made a regular regiment of the British Army. It fought in no engagements during the war, and disbanded at the peace.

Newfoundland Volunteers

Raised in St. John's Newfoundland in October 1779 by Maj. Robert Pringle as a volunteer militia unit to help defend the province. The corps entertained 360 men, but served less than a year. It was disbanded in 1780, with the raising of the Newfoundland Regiment.

New Hampshire Volunteers
also known as Stark's Corps

Raised in New York City and Philadelphia by Maj. William Stark of New Hampshire, who had commanded a company of Rogers' Rangers during the French and Indian War. William Stark was the older brother of Rebel Gen. John Stark, the hero of the battle of Bennington. Stark, originally a Rebel became dissatisfied with the way he was treated. So he went to British-occupied New York and offered his military services. The bulk of the corps was drafted in the summer of 1777 into the Queen's American Rangers in New Jersey. Later recruits were drafted into the 2nd Battalion, New Jersey Volunteers and the King's Orange Rangers. Several officers joined the Guides and Pioneers.

New Jersey Loyalist Military Units

Cortland Skinner, the last attorney general under the Royal government of New Jersey, was commissioned a brigadier general by Lt. Gen. William Howe in September 1776 and empowered to raise a brigade of six battalions to be known as the New Jersey Volunteers. The Volunteers would become the largest Provincial unit raised during the war, with more than 3,300 officers and men eventually serving at one time or another. Losses in battle and the incomplete state of the battalions led to two reductions during the war. On April 25, 1778 the 1st and 5th Battalions were combined together, as well as the 3rd and 6th Battalions; the 4th Battalions was reorganized from ten companies to five, while the 2nd Battalion (then attached to the Royal Artillery) was unaffected. On 27 July 1781, the 2nd Battalion was drafted into the 1st and 4th Battalions; the 3rd Battalion was renumbered as the new 2nd Battalion, and the 4th as the new 3rd Battalion.

New Jersey Militia

During the initial British occupation of New Jersey, there was only one attempt to reorganize the militia on behalf of the Crown. In December 1776, the militia of Monmouth County (which contained a large number of Loyalists) laid down its arms when the British advanced into the area. Some militia was then organized by Col. George Taylor, a former militia officer there. After the British pulled back the following month, the militia melted away. Col. Taylor remained within the British lines the remainder of the war, serving as a guide an unsuccessfully attempting to raise a Provincial company at Sandy Hook.

New Jersey Volunteers Light Dragoons

Raised in 1777 by Capt. Anthony Mosengeil. The troops only appear to have served during that year, and what became of the men is unknown. Mosengeil, a native of Germany, would go on to serve as major-of-brigade to the Anspach troops. Brig.

Gen. Skinner in 1780 contemplated raising four troops of light dragoons to attach to the brigade, but the plan was not accepted by Sir Henry Clinton.

Ist Battalion, New Jersey Volunteers

Raised on July 1, 1776 by Lt. Col. Elisha Lawrence, primarily from Loyalists in Monmouth County. The corps took part in the 1776 British invasion of New Jersey and for a time was stationed at New Brunswick. The battalion fought in August 1777 raid on Staten Island, 1778 raid on Egg Harbor, 1779 expedition to Middletown, 1780 raid on Staten Island, at Elizabethtown, Connecticut Farms, and Springfield in 1780, and Pleasant Valley in 1781. A detachment of men under Lt. John Taylor served in Patrick Ferguson's American Volunteers. A light infantry company was raised in 1780, commanded by Capt. James Shaw, which became a part of the Provincial Light Infantry. Upon the merger of the 1st and 5th Battalions on April 25, 1778, the corps was commanded by Lt. Col. Joseph Barton, who was later replaced by Lt. Col. Stephen DeLancey. The same year, the battalion received 34 drafts from the West Jersey Volunteers. The battalion was disbanded October 10, 1783 along the Saint John River.

2nd Battalion, New Jersey Volunteers

Established in November 1776 by Lt. Col. John Morris, a retired lieutenant of the British Army's 47th Regiment of Foot. Recruited primarily in Monmouth County, the corps lost its first engagement, on January 2, 1777, losing four soldiers killed and as many as 30 others captured near Freehold. In April 1777, to supplement the Royal Artillery's perpetual shortage of artillerymen, the battalion was attached to this corps, with which it would serve until November 1779. During that time it took part in the Philadelphia Campaign and the battle of Monmouth. After it returned to an infantry unit, it primarily garrisoned

Lloyd's Neck, Long Island. A detachment under Lt. William Stevenson served in Patrick Ferguson's American Volunteers. A light infantry company was formed in 1780 under Capt. Norman McLeod, which became a part of the Provincial Light Infantry. The battalion was drafted into the 1st and 4th New Jersey Volunteers on July 27, 1781.

3rd Battalion, New Jersey Volunteers

Commissioned in November 1776, this battalion was initially to be commanded by William Luce of Elizabethtown. The plan went awry due to his being taken prisoner. The new commander, Lt. Col. Edward Vaughan Dongan of Rahway, raised the battalion principally in Essex County. Dongan served until he was mortally wounded on August 22, 1777 during Sullivan's raid on Staten Island. Upon the merger of the 3rd and 6th Battalions on April 25, 1778, command passed to Lt. Col. Isaac Allen. In addition to Staten Island, the battalion fought at Egg Harbor and Savannah, Georgia in 1778; Briar Creek, Stono Ferry and the siege of Savannah in 1779; Musgrove's Mills, Augusta and Long Canes in 1780; Long Canes again, the siege of Ninety Six and Eutaw Springs in 1781, the two latter being the fiercest engagements of the unit. The battalion consisted of nine companies, two of which came from the West Jersey Volunteers in late September 1778. It was renumbered as the 2nd Battalion on July 27, 1781 and disbanded along the Saint John River on October 10, 1783.

4th Battalion, New Jersey Volunteers

Commissioned on November 16, 1776, this battalion was raised primarily in Bergen and Morris counties by Lt. Col. Abraham Van Buskirk of Teaneck. Organized initially into ten companies, this was reduced to five in the consolidation of April 25, 1778. The battalion participated in numerous raids in New Jersey in 1777, along with Sullivan's and Dickinson's raids on Staten Island, and Second River; they participated in Lord Cornwallis's

Bergen County Grand Forage in 1778; Closter, New Bridge, Little Ferry, Woodbridge, Middletown and Paulus Hook in 1779; Staten Island, Elizabethtown, Hopperstown, Connecticut Farms, and Springfield in 1780; plus Pleasant Valley and Fort Griswold in 1781. A detachment of the battalion under Capt. Samuel Ryerson made up nearly one quarter of Patrick Ferguson's American Volunteers. A light infantry company was raised in 1780, commanded by Capt. Jacob Van Buskirk, the colonel's son. This company became a part of the Provincial Light Infantry. The battalion was renumbered as the 3rd in the reorganization of July 27, 1781 and disbanded along the Saint John River on October 10, 1783.

5th Battalion, New Jersey Volunteers

Commissioned on November 27, 1777, this battalion was raised primarily in Sussex County by Lt. Col. Joseph Barton, a veteran of the Provincial Forces in the French and Indian War. Detachments from the unit took part on several raids in New Jersey before being surprised during Sullivan's raid on Staten Island, August 22, 1777, where Barton and upwards of thirty men were taken prisoner. The unit was merged into the 1st Battalion on April 25, 1778.

6th Battalion, New Jersey Volunteers

Commissioned on December 3, 1776, the final battalion of New Jersey Volunteers was commanded by Isaac Allen, a lawyer from Trenton. The men were recruited from Hunterdon County, including Trenton and Princeton. Washington's attack on these places slowed down recruiting and cost the battalion two officers. The battalion lost its second in command, Maj. Richard Witham Stockton, when he and 59 other New Jersey Volunteers were taken prisoner at Bennet's Neck, near New Brunswick, on February 18,1777. The second major of the unit, Maj. John Barnes of Trenton, was mortally wounded during Continental

Army Maj. Gen. John Sullivan's raid on Staten Island. As an under-strength unit, it was combined with the 3rd Battalion on April 25, 1778.

West Jersey Volunteers
Also known as the Independent New Jersey Volunteers

Drawn from the counties of Salem, Gloucester, and Cumberland, part of the old province of West Jersey, this Provincial corps was raised at Philadelphia in January 1778 by Maj. John Vandyke. In March, the embryonic unit established the post at Billingsport on the Delaware, from which it launched several incursions into the countryside. After the evacuation of Philadelphia, the corps helped construct batteries on Sandy Hook, in anticipation of a French fleet attack on New York. Shortly afterwards the corps was drafted into the 1st and 3rd Battalions of New Jersey Volunteers, and the British Legion.

New York Militia

After the British conquest of New York City and Long Island in 1776, Royal Governor William Tryon set about reorganizing the militia on Manhattan and the surrounding counties. By 1780, between inhabitants and refugees driven within the lines, the militia probably numbered in excess of 5,500 officers and men.

Anderson's Independent Company of Volunteers

Raised by Capt. James Anderson in November 1777. Served as an independent company of militia until embodied in the Loyal Volunteers of the City of New York in 1780.

Barrack Master General's Volunteers

Commanded by Joseph Page, the 91 officers and men in this company were drawn from this civil branch's department. Like other similar companies raised in the winter of 1779-1780, the unit was expected to defend their storehouse in the event of an attack on the city.

Brownjohn's Independent Company of Volunteers

Raised by Capt. Samuel Brownjohn in November 1777. Served as an independent company of militia until embodied in the Loyal Volunteers of the City of New York in 1780.

Chiltas' Independent Company of Volunteers

Raised by Capt. Robert Chiltas in November 1777. Served as an independent company of militia until embodied in the Loyal Volunteers of the City of New York in 1780.

Dickson's Independent Company of Volunteers

Raised by Capt. William Dickson in November 1777. Served as an independent company of militia until embodied in the Loyal Volunteers of the City of New York in 1780. Capt. Dickson died on July 9, 1780 while bathing in a pond near Jamaica, Long Island.

Engineer Volunteers

Raised from the Engineer's Department, this 134-man unit was commanded by Capt. Alexander Mercer of the Corps of Engineers. The unit served during the winter of 1779-1780 and was apparently disbanded within the next year or two.

German Independent Company of New York Militia

One of the original volunteer militia units organized after the fall of New York City in 1776. Commanded by Capt. Frederick William Hulet, the company appears to have been disbanded by January 1780.

King's County Militia

Commanded by William Axtell, a wealthy member of His Majesty's Council for New York who had been arrested by the Revolutionary authorities in 1776. The smallest of the Long Island militia units, the corps consisted of about 400 men, divided into seven infantry companies and one troop of light horse. It spent the war doing routine patrols and assisted in the construction of fortifications for the British, all in the neighborhood of Brooklyn.

King's Dock Yard Volunteers

Over 160 officers and men, led by William Fowler, composed this volunteer corps during the winter of 1779-1780. These men would defend the valuable shipyards in the event of a winter attack on the city.

Loyal Commissariat Volunteers

On November 2, 1779, two companies of men were raised out of the Commissary General's Department and placed under the command of Maj. William Butler. As a part of the New York City Militia establishment, the corps served until 1782.

Loyal Ordnance Volunteers

In January 1780, the men of the Royal Artillery's Ordnance Branch petitioned to be armed and join in the defense of New York City. Under the command of Capt. George Wray, along with three companies of seaman under the same appellation, the unit was made a part of the New York City Militia establishment.

Loyal Volunteers of the City of New York

Created in July 1780 by the joining of seven independent volunteer companies of New York City Militia. Uniformed at their own expense, the members of the corps were commanded by Lt. Col. David Mathews, the mayor of New York City. On July 2, 1781 the corps received "an elegant pair of colours" from New York governor and British Lt. Gen. James Robertson.

The episode was recorded by British Deputy Adjutant Gen. Frederick Mackenzie in his diary: "One of the Battalions of this City Militia is Commanded by Mr. David Mathews, the Mayor, and is Composed of the Merchants and traders of New York. Gen. Robertson, the Governor, having made them a present of a pair of Colours, they were out a few days ago to be reviewed by him, and some of the principal Officers, in describing what they could do, told him, they could, March, Wheel, form Columns, Retire, Advance, & *Charge*; 'Yes, Gentlemen' said the General, 'I am convinced you can *Charge* better than any Corps in His Majesty's service.'"

Massachusetts Volunteers

An independent company of militia raised at New York City by Capt. William Taylor in October 1777. Served as an independent company for the remainder of the war.

Mayor's Independent Company of Volunteers

Raised by the Mayor of New York, David Mathews, in November 1777 as a uniformed volunteer militia company. Capt. Mathews was promoted to lieutenant colonel upon the joining of the different volunteer companies in July 1780.

McAdam's Independent Company of Volunteers

Raised by Capt. John Loudon McAdam on November 4, 1777. Served as an independent company of militia until embodied in the Loyal Volunteers of the City of New York in 1780. Born in Scotland, McAdam sailed to New York as a youth and lived with his uncle in New York City. During the Revolutionary War, he was the commissioner for prize ships captured by the Royal Navy and British privateers. He offered more than 450 ships

John Loudon McAdam

for auction, collecting fees for those he sold. Those fees provided some of the basis for his fortune when he moved back to Scotland, bought land, got involved in local road-building, invented a new paving process—and gave the world "macadamized" roads.

McDonald's Company of Volunteers

This New York City Militia unit was composed primarily of Highlander refugees from North Carolina. Under the command of Capt. Allan McDonald of the Royal Highland Emigrants, it is unknown what became of the company after he left it in 1778.

New York City Militia

Within weeks of the British taking possession of New York City, a regiment of city militia was organized under Col. George Brewerton, also serving as commander of the 2nd Battalion, DeLancey's Brigade. The following year, 1777, the volunteer companies were loosely combined into a battalion under Col. William Waddell. Neither arrangement appears to have been satisfactory, and in the winter of 1779-1780, all able-bodied males between the ages of seventeen to sixty were to be enrolled in the militia, excluding Quakers, firemen, and those then serving in volunteer companies. Forming forty "city companies," they were organized that summer into four battalions, commanded by Lt. Colonels William Walton, Alexander Wallace, Isaac Low, and Philip Kearney respectively. These battalions mustered 2,662 officers and men by February 1780. The militia did duty into 1783, and then became defunct as the city was evacuated.

New York Independent Highland Volunteers

One of the original volunteer militia units organized after the fall of New York City in 1776. Commanded by Capt. Normand Tolmie, these Highlanders served as an independent company of New York City Militia for the remainder of the war.

New York Marine Company of Artillery

Formed in October 1779, this 98-man company was raised from New York's nautical community and commanded by Capt. Vincent Pearce Ashfield, president of the New York Marine Society. Over half the company. came from the nautical community, which was "acquainted with the management of cannon." The unit was raised to defend possible French naval attacks on the port or a siege of the city.

New York Rangers
also known as the First
Independent Company of Rangers

One of the first independent volunteer companies of New York City Militia, this 110-man unit was commanded by Capt. Christopher Benson. The Volunteers served as guards at various parts of the city. It participated in one action during the war, a small 1777 raid into neighboring Bergen County, New Jersey.

New York Volunteers
also known as the New York Companies
and the 3ʳᵈ American Regiment

Amongst the very first Provincial units raised, and the first of the Hudson River Valley. The unit initially consisted of two independent companies raised in January 1776 by Captains Alexander Grant and Archibald Campbell, both of whom would by killed in action in 1777. They took part in the New York Campaign, including the battles of Brooklyn, White Plains, and Fort Washington. In 1777, they were noted for their assaults at Ward's House in March and Fort Montgomery the following October. After the last-mentioned action, the corps was commanded by Lt. Col. George Turnbull who would lead it for the remainder of the war. The unit was expanded by the addition of the 1ˢᵗ Duchess County Company commanded by Capt. John

Howard, and newly-raised companies. The unit sailed south with the expedition to take Georgia under Lt. Col. Archibald Campbell of the 71st Regiment, taking part in the capture (and later defense) of Savannah, Briar Creek, Stono Ferry, the siege of Charleston, Rocky Mount, Hobkirk's Hill, and Eutaw Springs. A light infantry company under Capt. John Coffin was converted to cavalry in September 1780. The regiment was put on the American Establishment as the 3rd American Regiment in early 1780. After the evacuation of Charleston, the corps served at New York until leaving for the Saint John River, where it was disbanded on October 10, 1783.

Quarter Master General's Volunteers

Commanded by Maj. Henry Bruen, this 50-man company, raised in the winter of 1779-1780, was drawn from the civil branch that bore its name. In the event of an attack on the city, they were expected to defend the stores in their department's trust.

Queens County Militia

The most active of the Long Island militia units. Commanded by Col. Archibald Hamilton from his manor estate of Innerwick, the corps consisted of more than a dozen companies of infantry and three troops of light horse, totaling over a thousand men. Queens had the most active Loyalist population of the area, prompting the state authorities to disarm the inhabitants in February 1776. The militia would provide numerous guards along the shores and maintain a fort at Whitestone. They took part in numerous skirmishes throughout the war, helping to repel whaleboat raids from Connecticut and assisting in two British troops movements to the east end of the island.

Richmond County Militia

Staten Island's militia was commanded by Col. Christopher Billopp, whose handsome estate still stands in the Tottenville section of the island. Upon the British landing in early July 1776, the militia of the island was mustered by Governor William Tryon and the corps started service; the regiment's troop of light horse, commanded by Capt. Isaac Decker, even provided guard for Lt. Gen. William Howe. The unit provided the typical guards and patrols for the island, likewise helping in the construction of fortifications. Detachments helped repel different Rebel incursions on the island. They also took part in one raid in 1781, to Trembly's Point, New Jersey.

Skinner's Independent Company of Volunteers

Raised by Capt., later Maj., Stephen Skinner of New Jersey in November 1777. Served as an independent company of militia until embodied in the Loyal Volunteers of the City of New York in 1780.

Suffolk County Militia

Commanded by Col. Richard Floyd, owner of a 500-acre farm in Brookhaven (now Mastic), Long Island. The most extensive area of Long Island was also the least loyal to the British. The most active of the militia was centered in the Huntington area, near the outpost of Lloyd's Neck. On a visit to the county in August 1778, Governor William Tryon tendered the oath of allegiance to some 2,677 inhabitants, who ostensibly were liable for militia service. In reality, the number who actually served was considerably lower. Detachments of the unit did guard duty to detect whaleboat raids from Connecticut.

Templeton's Independent Company of Volunteers

Raised by Capt. Oliver Templeton in November 1777. Served as an independent company of militia until embodied in the Loyal Volunteers of the City of New York in 1780.

Westchester Chasseurs

This 1777 troop of volunteer militia cavalry consisted of the "elite of the county" and commanded by Capt. James DeLancey, colonel of the militia and high sheriff of Westchester County. While the officers and men were drawn from the militia, this embodied troop was only to serve for about the final four months of 1777. Unlike the rest of the militia, this troop of 50 men was provided with arms and equipage by the British. These items were returned to the British when the troop was disbanded on November 3, 1777. It had fought in only a couple minor skirmishes during its tenure.

Westchester County Militia
also known as DeLancey's Refugees

Initially mustered by Governor William Tryon In November 1776, the corps became one of the most effective of all Loyalist units. Commanded by Col. James DeLancey until his capture in

James DeLancey
Early Manhattan Island

November 1777. In his absence, Maj. Mansfield Baremore and Lt. Col. Isaac Hatfield. Col. DeLancey resumed command upon his exchange in early 1780 and rapidly expanded the corps to resemble a legion of light infantry and cavalry. Between the end of 1779 and May of 1782, the corps captured some 466 officers and men, many of them Continentals. They received great praise for their attack on a Continental Army outpost in Westchester called Young's House in 1780 and the defeat of the Rhode Island Regiment, a unit consisting in large part of ex-slaves, at Croton, New York. During the time of the French and American 1781 incursion near the lines at Kingsbridge, the 490 men of the militia were subsisted by the British, one of the few times in the war this occurred. Unlike the other New York Militias, the corps as a whole embarked for Nova Scotia in June 1783, settling in Cumberland County.

Williams' Independent Company of Volunteers

Raised by Capt. Thomas Charles Williams in November 1777. Served as an independent company of militia until embodied in the Loyal Volunteers of the City of New York in 1780.

Norfolk Regiment, Virginia Militia

Among the units serving in 1775/76 under Virginia's governor, Lord Dunmore, was this militia regiment, commanded by Col. Alexander Gordon. Some members took part in the engagement at Great Bridge in December 1775. After the evacuation of the province in 1776, it ceased to exist.

North Carolina Highlanders

Authorized on August 1, 1780. Governor Josiah Martin of North Carolina, with the Provincial rank of lieutenant colonel, attempted to recruit a battalion of Highlanders from amongst the province's large Scottish population. While this happened easily in 1776 when the North Carolina Provincials had been raised, times had changed in the ensuing four years. Many of the

Scots who had taken part in that campaign had either moved on to other corps or could not be persuaded to leave home. Officers for a full battalion were commissioned, although only about 115 men were enlisted, formed into two companies. Lt. Col. Allan Stewart, captain of the Black Pioneers, took field command of the unit. After spending 1782 doing garrison duty around Charleston, that October the effective men were formed into a new company and added to the Royal North Carolina Regiment.

North Carolina Independent Company

Prior to, and during the initial phases of Lord Cornwallis's invasion of North Carolina, the British explored the idea of raising independent Provincial companies in lieu of new regiments, probably with an eye toward joining them to existing corps. Most of these companies failed to get off the ground, with the exception of one commanded by Capt. Eli Branson, a former officer of the North Carolina Provincials. The company accompanied Cornwallis into Virginia, where it was a part of the army captured at Yorktown. After their exchange, they remained at New York until disbanded later along the Saint John River.

North Carolina Independent Dragoons
also known as Wilmington Light Dragoons, and North Carolina Light Dragoons

Unit was raised in 1781 at Wilmington, North Carolina by Capt. John Gordon, who was killed in action near New Bern on August 19, 1781. His successor, Capt. Robert Gillies, was killed in a skirmish at Biggin Bridge South Carolina, on 29 August 1782. The troop was thereafter incorporated into the South Carolina Royalists. When raised, they were described by the commander at Wilmington as "an exceeding pretty troop" with no man above 23 years of age.

North Carolina Militia

Prior to the 1781 British invasion of the province, militia service for North Carolina's Loyalists was mostly limited to joining Patrick Ferguson during his brief time in Tryon County, shortly before the battle of King's Mountain. While some militia became a part of Cornwallis' force traveling through the province in 1781, such as that under Lt. Col. James Hunter, others were intercepted en route, such as was the case in the disastrous defeat of Col. John Pyle and his men at the hands of Lee's Legion and others. The main task of organizing the province's militia fell to the British commander at Wilmington, Maj. James Henry Craig. Craig issued commissions based on the traditional county method, with regiments being raised in Anson, Bladen, Cumberland, Orange, Chatham, and Randolph. The absence of Cornwallis' army actually encouraged more Loyalists to take up arms, led by such active leaders as Colonels David Fanning and Hector McNeil, Sr. The high-water mark for the militia came on September 13, 1781, when 1,100 men captured Hillsborough, taking numerous military and political prisoners. The evacuation of Wilmington the following November greatly diminished, but did not eliminate, all militia activity in the province. Many of the militia did, however leave with Maj. Craig. These men were organized into a regiment under Col. Samuel Campbell, serving on James Island, South Carolina for most of 1782.

North Carolina Provincials

On January 10, 1776, Governor Josiah Martin of North Carolina authorized one of the largest Loyalist uprisings of the war. In expectation of a British expedition led by Lt. Gen. Henry Clinton, the Loyalists were to embody and await his arrival to receive arms and ammunition that he was expected to bring. Gov. Martin appointed Maj. Donald MacDonald of the 1st Battalion, Royal Highland Emigrants as brigadier general of his troops, who were principally composed of Highlanders and Loyalists. Colonels were appointed to raise regiments, along with many captains of both foot and horse. Indeed, more troops were raised than there were arms on hand to equip them; of the 1,400 infantry embodied in five weeks time, only 650 were armed with muskets or rifles. Rising prematurely, the troops marched on until February 27, 1776 when it was decided to attack the enemy occupying Moore's Creek Bridge. With 800 men, and a battle cry of "King George and Broadswords" the attack was to commence with "Three cheers, the Drum to beat, and the Pipes to play." The attack was a disaster, with the two captains leading the charge shot down, along with most of their men. With no remaining food, or order, the corps disintegrated. Those who did not escape home were taken, including most of the officers, including Donald McDonald. Some of the officers would go on to serve in the Royal North Carolina Regiment, North Carolina Highlanders or other units later on. A number of survivors made their way north and helped form the Highland Company of the Queen's American Rangers.

North Carolina Volunteers

Raised from recruits who had fought at Ramsaur's (Ramsour's) Mills, North Carolina on June 20, 1780, this embodied volunteer militia unit was commanded by Col. Samuel Bryan. Unlike other militia corps, the unit was in constant service, serving primarily in South Carolina, where it took a major part in the 1780 battles of Hanging Rock and Camden. Two companies of the corps were recruited along Lord Cornwallis' march through North Carolina in 1781, eventually surrendering with him at Yorktown. The remainder was disbanded in South Carolina by the evacuation in December 1782.

Nova Scotia Militia

The defense of England's northernmost colony on the Atlantic coast centered initially on a very small garrison of troops in Halifax. Governor Francis Legge, a former lieutenant colonel of the 55th Regiment of Foot, took steps in 1775 to organize the province's militia to aid in that defense. Regiments, companies and troops were organized in Annapolis, Colchester, Cumberland, Halifax, Hants, King's, Lunenburg, Queen's, and Sunbury. The primary duty of these corps, especially those along the coast, was to defend their towns against New England privateers. In this they were generally unsuccessful; however in at least two instances in the winter of 1780, Lunenburg Militia under Col. John Creighton successfully captured two vessels. The Halifax Regiment's light infantry company took part in offensive operations in 1777, as a part of the expedition to clear out the Saint John River Valley of rebels and disaffected Acadians. At the end of hostilities, Sir Guy Carleton organized civilian refugees embarking for Nova Scotia into "militia companies" which were numbered, based on their destination. These commissions were to last until refugees were better organized and integrated by the government of Nova Scotia.

Nova Scotia Volunteers

This corps, raised in 1775 by Governor Francis Legge, went through two incarnations. When originally raised, it fell under the control of the governor and government of Nova Scotia. In June 1776, when the whole British Army was briefly in Halifax, the corps was restructured as a Provincial unit. Later recruiting in Newfoundland greatly expanded the size of the corps, which was made complete by the addition of Timothy Hierlihy's Independent Companies. The corps primarily performed garrison duty in the Halifax area until it was disbanded on October 10, 1783.

Pennsylvania Loyalists

William Allen raised the unit in October 1777. Allen, from a prominent Pennsylvania family, was one of the first officers commissioned by the Continental Congress and took part in the Continental Army's invasion of Canada in 1775, as lieutenant colonel of the 2nd Pennsylvania Battalion. But when Congress declared independence, he resigned his commission on July 24, 1776 and, as a Loyalist lieutenant colonel, raised and commanded the Pennsylvania Loyalists. Along with the Maryland Loyalists, the unit embarked from New York in November 1778 for West Florida. After a brief stop at Jamaica, the corps arrived at Pensacola the following January, where it did garrison duty for the next few years. As with the Maryland Loyalists, smallpox quickly swept through the corps, greatly diminishing its ranks. As a result of this, the garrison commander, Gen. John Campbell, merged the two Provincial units into the United Corps of Pennsylvania and Maryland Loyalists. Sir Henry Clinton reversed this decision and the two corps resumed life as independent regiments. In 1781, the unit took part in the unsuccessful assault on the Village of Mobile and siege of Pensacola. During the latter, 45 men of the corps were instantly killed when a Spanish shell struck the magazine of the fort where the Pennsylvanians were just in the act of receiving ammunition. It was the largest loss of life of any Provincial unit in any battle of the war. The survivors spent the next year on parole in New York, and afterwards in garrison there until the conclusion of hostilities. The unit was disbanded along the Saint John River on October 10, 1783.

Pepperell's Corps

Sir William Pepperell, who raised and commanded this corps, lived in Jamaica Plains, outside of Boston. After fleeing an anti-Loyalist mob, he enrolled "in an association for the defense" but did not take up arms. He departed for England in 1775 and became president of a Loyalist association there. This association became the nucleus of a volunteer company of between fifty and eighty American exiles in London. They were just one of many similar volunteer associations raised in England in 1779 after fears of a French invasion. The company probably dissolved before the end of the war.

Pfister's Corps of Royalists
also known as the Loyal Volunteers

Another of the "Royalist" units raised during the Burgoyne Campaign. Francis Pfister of Hoosick, an old lieutenant from the 60th Regiment during the French and Indian War, commenced clandestinely recruiting officers and men in July 1777 in anticipation of the army under Burgoyne advancing towards his neighborhood. The corps only started to form together the day before the battle of Bennington, in which action Pfister and 19 men of the corps were killed, and another 190 taken prisoner. Of the 370 officers and men recruited during the campaign, 27 were left to surrender at Saratoga, but 117 others escaped to Canada under their new commander, Capt. Samuel Mackay. Mackay, who had commanded one of the Canadian Companies, was not a favorite of Sir Guy Carleton, and only lasted in command until 1778, when Capt. Robert Leake took charge of the corps. A detachment of the most fit of the unit was selected and often referred to as an independent company under Leake. This company did take part in several large expeditions into New York over the next several years. The corps passed out of existence in November 1781 when it became a part of the new Loyal Rangers. Robert Leake, however went on to join the King's Royal Regiment of New York.

Philadelphia Light Dragoons

Raised as two Independent troops, the first in November 1777 by Capt. Richard Hovenden, the second the following January by

Capt. Jacob James. Each troop took part in several forays out of Philadelphia that winter, as well as the battle of Crooked Billet on May 4, 1778. On August 1, 1778, the two troops, along with Kinloch's Light Dragoons, became the initial cavalry portion of the British Legion, ending their tenure as independent units.

Prince of Wales American Volunteers

Raised by Brig. Gen. Montfort Browne, governor of the Bahama Islands, this regiment was to be the nucleus of a brigade of troops raised primarily in Connecticut and New England. Recruited at New York over the winter of 1776-1777, this Provincial unit took part in the 1777 battle of Danbury, Connecticut. The following year it was a part of the garrison of Rhode Island, where it took part in the siege. After returning to New York in 1779, it provided 29 men under Capt. Charles McNeill to the American Volunteers. The rest of the corps would join those men at the siege of Charleston, sailing there with the April reinforcement from New York. The corps took the brunt of the assault at the August 6, 1780 battle of Hanging Rock, South Carolina, losing five officers killed and scores of men. The regiment never recovered from the loss of so many men, serving in detachment form only for the remaining two years in South Carolina. The light infantry company of the corps fought at Cowpens, where most were taken prisoner. Those who survived were added to a new troop of the British Legion. The corps was mostly commanded in the field by its lieutenant colonel, first Thomas Pattinson, then Stephen DeLancey and finally Gabriel DeVeber. The corps returned to New York on the evacuation of Charleston in December 1782 where it served until disbanded along the Saint John River on October 10, 1783.

Provincial Light Infantry

Six companies of light infantry were joined together in August 1780 for the express purpose of creating a corps for an adventurous British officer, Lt. Col. John Watson Tadswell Watson of the Brigade of Guards. The unit was a part of Maj. Gen. Alexander Leslie's expedition to Virginia, which soon after was forwarded on to Charleston. During the winter and spring of 1781, the corps roamed the "High Hills of Santee" in pursuit of the partisan Thomas Sumter, defeating him several times. The unit fought in the bloody battle of Eutaw Springs on September 8, 1781, its last major action. Sent back to New York in the spring of 1782, where the companies were returned to their corps. The company from the King's American Regiment had been previously returned to its regiment, then serving in Georgia.

Quebec Militia

The principal Canadian contribution to the British cause came in the form of its militia. The militia should best be divided by those of the cities of Quebec and Montreal, and those of the countryside. The Quebec City Militia during the time of the 1775-1776 siege was composed of two regiments, one of French and one of English. At this time, the English regiment consisted of six companies commanded by Lt. Col. Henry Caldwell, with a strength of 296 rank and file; the French regiment had nine companies, including one of artillery, commanded by Col. Noël Voyer, with a strength of 572 officers and men. Both regiments would increase after the siege. The Montreal Regiment, commanded by Col. Dufils Desaunior, had a strength of 559 officers and men in 1778. The countryside militia, that composing the districts of Quebec, Montreal, and Three Rivers, boasted about 15,000 officers and men in 1778. Essentially, all the country militia could do was help to prevent desertions, manage some logistics and supply, and provide men for unpaid labor in groups called corvées.

Queen's American Rangers
also known as the Iˢᵗ American Regiment

The unit (named in honor of Queen Charlotte, the wife of King George III) was raised in August 1776 by Lt. Col. Robert Rogers, the famous ranger officer of the French and Indian War. Rogers issued warrants to scores of potential officers, not many of whom were to the British liking. As a result of numerous excesses and irregularities, Rogers and some 27 officers were dismissed from the service, without trial. The corps passed to the command of several British officers, the last of whom was Maj., later Lt. Col. John Graves Simcoe. Many of the new officers were those who had formerly served under Lord Dunmore in Virginia. The regiment became one of the most active Provincial regiments of the war, fighting at Mamaroneck, the British invasion of New Jersey, Brandywine, Germantown, Quintin's Bridge, Hancock's Bridge, Crooked Billet, Monmouth, Somerset, Staten Island, the siege of Charleston, Hopperstown, Connecticut Farms, Springfield, Richmond, Petersburg, Spencer's Ordinary, Osborne's Landing

and finally Yorktown. A troop of cavalry under Capt. John Saunders took part in Leslie's Virginia expedition, later serving at Georgetown, South Carolina. In early 1780, the corps had the honor of being put on the American Establishment as the 1st American Regiment, and on December 25, 1782, a regular regiment of the British Army. After spending its final days at New York, the corps was disbanded along the Saint John River on October 10, 1783. Simcoe became the first Lieutenant

John Graves Simcoe
Government of Ontario Art Collection

Governor of Upper Canada. The modern Queen's York Rangers of the Canadian Militia descends directly from this unit, and is still sometimes styled the 1st American Regiment.

Queen's Loyal Rangers

The second of the so-called Royalist corps, this unit was raised on May 28, 1777 by Lt. Col. John Peters of Vermont. Recruiting during the course of the Burgoyne Campaign, more than 330 officers and men were soon raised, but just as quickly lost or dissipated by death, desertion, detachment, transfer, or capture. The corps particularly lost a number of men at Bennington on August 16, 1777. After the battle of Saratoga, the remainder of the corps shared the limbo in Quebec experienced by all the Royalist units. Never having received proper commissions from Sir Guy Carleton or Burgoyne, they were considered as merely unattached groups of men by the new commander, Lt. Gen. Frederick Haldimand. After spending years on years on non-military duties or as marines or artificers, the corps was merged with the other Royalist units on November 25, 1781 to form the Provincial regiment of Loyal Rangers.

Queen's Own
Loyal Virginia Regiment

Raised in November 1775 as a result of Virginia Governor Lord Dunmore's proclamation calling forth the assistance of Loyalists. The unit, commanded by Lt. Col. Jacob Ellegood, took part in the battle of Great Bridge on December 9, 1775 and a few weeks later at Norfolk. As a non-Provincial unit, all the expenses of the corps were paid by the Government of Virginia, through the British Treasury. After spending much of the first half of 1776 on board Dunmore's shipping or on Gwynn's Island, the troops evacuated Virginia to join the British at New York. The corps was disbanded on Staten Island in August 1776. Many of the officers would go on to later serve in the Queen's American Rangers.

Queen's Royal Rangers

Unlike the royal governors in New England, the governor of Virginia, John Murray, the Earl of Dunmore, decided to fight the Rebels in his state. In November 1775, Dunmore authorized a regiment styled the Queen's Royal Rangers, to be raised by enlisting Loyalists and Indians "in the back parts and Canada." For his new regiment's commander, he chose John Connolly and made him a lieutenant colonel. Connolly, a nephew of a British Indian agent, lived in what had been Fort Pitt (future site of Pittsburgh and, for a while, dubbed Fort Dunmore). The governor believed that an expedition by the Rangers would conquer the western territory, which Dunmore envisioned as a future addition to Virginia. But within days after creation of the regiment, Rebels arrested Connolly in Hagerstown, Maryland, on his way to Detroit. He carried incriminating documents showing what Dunmore planned. Connolly would remain a prisoner through 1780. On his exchange, he would raise the Loyal Foresters at New York.

Reid's Independent
North Carolina Company

A colonel in the North Carolina Militia and captain in Gov. Josiah Martin's North Carolina Provincials, Thomas McDonald Reid escaped the disaster of the February 1776 battle of Moore's Creek Bridge. The following May, Gov. Martin commissioned Reid captain of an independent company, presumably filled by fellow survivors of the battle who escaped capture. The company probably met up with Lt. Gen. Henry Clinton's small expedition to North Carolina that spring, but otherwise did little. The company appears to have been disbanded at New York, on or about November 24, 1776.

Robins' Company of Partisans

Raised in 1781 by Capt. Nathaniel Robins, this Refugee company successfully operated several whaleboats out of Staten Island, raiding the New Jersey shore.

Roman Catholic Volunteers

One of the most unusual Provincial regiments. The corps, authorized in October 1777, was "to Consist of Roman Catholicks only on a presumption that they will prefer serving under an Officer to whom they are naturally attached..." That officer would be Lt. Col. Alfred Clifton, an inhabitant of Philadelphia. While the corps fought in no major battle, it would raise some 300 officers and men. Discipline among the officers was a problem, with two captains being cashiered for an altercation with each other on the regimental parade. After death and desertion had reduced its size, and with little prospect of completing the unit after the evacuation of Philadelphia, many men were drafted primarily into the Volunteers of Ireland, with others going to the British Legion, DeLancey's Brigade and Pennsylvania Loyalists.

Royal American Reformees

This Provincial regiment was authorized in April 1778 in a first attempt to exclusively recruit Continental Army deserters into a corps for British service. The unit was the brainchild of Lt. Col. Rudolphus Ritzema, who had served the Continental Army as colonel of the 1st New York Regiment during the 1776 Canadian Campaign. Ritzema served thereafter in the New York City Campaign, when he appears to have gone over to the British. The Reformees consisted of four companies, and only attracted some 125 officers and men. They never fought in a battle and as an under-strength regiment were drafted in September 1778. Some were formed into a company for the British Legion, under the command of John B. Scott, formerly a captain in the 2nd New Jersey Continentals, while others went to the Queen's American Rangers and DeLancey's Brigade. The unit's major, James Rogers, would go on to command the 2nd Battalion, King's American Rangers.

Royal Fencible Americans
also known as the Royal Fencible American Regiment

The plan for forming this unit, as a six-company corps of light infantry, was proposed by Joseph Goreham shortly before hostilities broke out in America. (The term *fencible* ["in defense of"] means that the unit can be deployed only on home territory.) Goreham, a former commander of Rangers in Nova Scotia during the previous war, arrived at Boston in the fall of 1775, meeting up with officers already recruiting for the corps. Over the next year, the unit would recruit extensively in Nova Scotia, Newfoundland and the Island of Saint John's (later Prince Edward) Island. On May 24, 1776, Lt. Col. Goreham and the Fencibles left Halifax for Fort Cumberland, where the bulk of the corps would spend the next seven and a half years. Fort Cumberland, located at the head of the Bay of Fundy, would be the scene of one of the first invasions launched by the United States, a modest effort to attempt an insurrection in Nova Scotia and have it join in the Revolution. A force of some 200 New Englanders, Acadians, and Indians at the end of October 1776 arrived before Fort Cumberland and lay siege to it. After weeks without provoking the hoped-for uprising, the besiegers, under Jonathan Eddy, were routed by a sally from the fort and reinforcements arriving by sea from Halifax. The corps afterwards provided a detachment that took part in the 1777 expedition up the Saint John River to drive away and disarm any remnants of the Eddy Rebellion, as the previous year's encounter came to be known. They likewise constructed and garrisoned Fort Howe at the mouth of the river, which post would later become the site of the City of Saint John. The corps was disbanded on October 10, 1783 and drew land in Passamaquoddy.

Royal Highland Emigrants
Also known as the 84th Regiment of Foot and Young Royal Highlanders

Like the Fencible Americans, the plan for raising the Royal Highland Emigrants predated Lexington and Concord. The idea, proposed by Allan Maclean in March 1775, called for secretly associating new emigrants from Scotland to America to take

up arms on behalf of the British in the event of hostilities. Events in Massachusetts overtook this plan, but the concept of raising Scottish settlers remained, resulting in this two-battalion Provincial corps. On December 25, 1778, after heavy solicitation to the King and War Office by the officers, the corps was made a part of the regular British Army and numbered the 84th Regiment of Foot. More than 1,800 officers and men served in the regiment.

Allan Maclean

1st Battalion, Royal Highland Emigrants

Authorized by Lt. Gen. Thomas Gage on June 13. 1775, what would become the 1st battalion of the new corps was commanded by Lt. Col. Allan Maclean, a long-serving veteran of previous wars. The battalion would be primarily recruited from amongst disbanded Highlanders from the French and Indian War, living in Quebec and New York's Mohawk Valley. Other detachments and recruits would come from New York, the Island of Saint John, Philadelphia, and North Carolina. The 1st battalion's major, Donald McDonald, also served as brigadier general to the North Carolina Provincials before the disaster at Moore's Creek Bridge in February 1776. As many as seventy men of the 1st battalion were taken prisoner there, along with McDonald. After losing a detachment at the fall of St. John's in November 1775, the bulk of the battalion formed the nucleus of the British garrison at Quebec during the ensuing siege and assault of that place. From that point, through its disbandment in June 1784, the corps performed garrison duty throughout Quebec, providing detachments from time to time for different raids in New York.

2nd Battalion, Royal Highland Emigrants

Created at Boston the same time as the 1st battalion, this unit was led by Maj., later Lt. Col., John Small, a captain in the British 21st Regiment of Foot. This battalion was raised primarily in Nova Scotia, Newfoundland, Boston, New York, New Jersey, Philadelphia and South Carolina. The bulk of the battalion would perform garrison duty throughout the war at Fort Edward and Halifax, Nova Scotia. A detachment took part in the 1777 expedition up the Saint John River. Five companies of the battalion were transferred to New York City in 1779, with the flank companies taking part in the 1780 siege of Charleston. The five companies took part in Gen. Leslie's 1780 expedition to Virginia and subsequent transfer to Charleston. There the unit took part in numerous skirmishes, culminating in the battle of Eutaw Springs. On the evacuation of Charleston, these troops would sail for Jamaica, where they would remain in garrison until August of 1783. Returning first to New York, and then Nova Scotia, the battalion would be disbanded as opportunity offered: those in Nova Scotia on October 10, 1783, those returning from Jamaica the following month, and finally in April 1784 a company which had spent the bulk of the war in Newfoundland.

Royal North British Volunteers

Drawn primarily from Scottish merchants of Boston, many of whom were already serving in the Loyal American Association, this company was raised on October 29, 1775 and commanded by Capt. James Anderson. Their duty stations included an alarm post near Faneuil Hall. They were ordered to "Patrole the Streets within a certain District" and "take into Custody all Suspicious & Disorderly Persons found in the Streets at improper Hours." The company was disbanded in March 1776 upon the evacuation of Boston.

Royal North Carolina Regiment

Raised at Savannah by Lt. Col. John Hamilton in February 1779 from some of the survivors who had fought at Kettle Creek, Georgia. Initially set up as a combined infantry-cavalry unit, this Provincial regiment was all foot by the time of the siege of Savannah, in which it served. In 1780, it took part in the siege of Charleston, after which it greatly expanded in size, taking in recruits as well from the action at Ramsaur's Mills. The corps was a part of the bloody action at Hanging Rock and soon thereafter a part of the brigade under Lord Rawdon at the battle of Camden. In 1781 it accompanied Lord Cornwallis into North Carolina but the bulk remained at Wilmington when his Lordship advanced into Virginia. However, a reinforced light infantry company under Lt. Col. Hamilton did form a part of the army going to Virginia, to which would be added a new company of the regiment raised by Capt. William Chandler. This detachment would surrender at Yorktown the following October. The remainder of the regiment returned to Charleston in December 1781, following the evacuation of Wilmington. While at Charleston, the North Carolina Highlanders would be joined into the corps. After spending most of 1783 as part of the garrison of St. Augustine, the corps sailed to Country Harbor, Nova Scotia, where it was disbanded. More than 1,000 officers and men served in the corps at one time or another.

Saint John's Parish Volunteers

Commanded by Capt. Thomas Commander, this company of South Carolina Militia, often referred to as one of guides, served from 1780-1782. Commander was described by his superiors as an "active and zealous" officer.

Saint John's Volunteers

This small Provincial company was raised in February 1777 by Capt. Phillips Callbeck to garrison the Island of Saint John's, modern Prince Edward Island. With an authorized strength of 110 officers and men, it never reached half that number. Ordered disbanded in 1778 upon the arrival of Timothy Hierlihy's Independent Companies, the unit successfully lobbied Lord George Germain, British Secretary of State for America, to continue in existence for the remainder of the conflict. Never having left home or fought in a skirmish, the company was disbanded at the end of the war and received land grants on the island.

Sharp's Refugee Marines

This company advertised for recruits in 1779 and was commanded by Capt. Joseph Sharp. Probably meant to serve with the shipping of the Loyal Associated Refugees out of Newport, Rhode Island.

Smyth's Independent Company of Provincials
Also known as the Royal Hunters

This Provincial company of about 120 men was raised in September 1777 by Capt. John Ferdinand Dalziel Smyth, who had formerly served under Lord Dunmore in Virginia.

The company was attached to the Queen's American Rangers on October 16, 1777 and permanently incorporated into them thereafter.

South Carolina Independent Light Dragoons

Raised in 1781 on the Provincial establishment, this troop was commanded by Capt. Archibald Campbell. Campbell was killed January 3, 1782 at Videau's Bridge, South Carolina, after the troop had become a part of the South Carolina Royalists.

South Carolina Independent Volunteers

This unit was a loosely organized corps of no less than four troops of light horse, commanded by Maj. Andrew Cumming of South Carolina. These troops, which appear to have acted independent of each other, served on South Carolina's Militia establishment from 1781 to 1782.

South Carolina Light Dragoons

Two separate Provincial troops bore this name. The first was commanded by Capt. Edward Fenwick, a colonel in the Loyalist South Carolina Militia. Raised in January 1781, the troop fought near Pocotaligo in March and April of that year. Capt. Fenwick and most of the troop were taken prisoner there on April 13, 1781. The troop was exchanged and continued as an independent until through 1781. Afterwards the troop was incorporated into the South Carolina Royalists. A second troop was created shortly afterwards by taking men from each of the three Hessian regiments in garrison at Charleston and put under the command of Capt. Freidrich Starckloff. In order to draw the additional pay of cavalry and receive appropriate clothing, the British made this troop a part of the Provincial establishment. A part of the troop was taken at the loss of Fort Motte on May 12, 1781. The troop appears to have been disbanded and the men returned to their corps at some time after June 24, 1781.

South Carolina Militia

After the fall of Charleston on May 12, 1780, Sir Henry Clinton appointed Patrick Ferguson as Inspector General of Militia and tasked him with organizing corps to assist in the defense of the province. During 1780, Lord Cornwallis, and in his name, Lt. Col. Nesbitt Balfour, along with Ferguson, would organize as many as 5,000 militia for British service. Many of these officers and men however would prove highly unreliable, having joined the British only when it seemed resistance was futile. Any Continental troops sent into the province caused insurrections anew and lessened the number of Loyalist militia. The disastrous defeat of Ferguson's militia at King's Mountain on October 7, 1780 only added to this defection. The militia was generally organized into regiments or independent companies by district or county, such as Ninety Six, Camden, Orangeburgh, Cheraws, Beaufort, Craven, and Berkley. Brig. Gen. Robert Cunningham of the Ninety Six District was the senior officer of militia. In detachments large and small, they fought in almost every skirmish or engagement in the province over the next two years. When the British retracted the lines to near Charleston, the militia from the countryside, now refugees, were reorganized into new regiments, along with two troops of "rifle hussars" commanded by Majors William Cunningham and William Young. The militia continued to do duty on James Island until the evacuation of Charleston in December 1782, when all units were disbanded.

South Carolina Rangers

Authorized on June 4, 1780, this mounted infantry unit was commanded by Maj. John Harrison and eventually recruited some 136 officers and men. The corps was particularly active throughout 1781, fighting at Fort Watson, Hobkirk's Hill and

Shubrick's Plantation. Numerous casualties reduced the size of the corps, leading to its being incorporated as a new troop in the South Carolina Royalists on December 25, 1781.

South Carolina Royalists

The very first Provincial unit authorized in the South. Command of the corps was given on May 26, 1778 to Col. Alexander Innes, the Inspector General of Provincial Forces. About 1,200 officers and men served in the corps.

Ist Battalion, South Carolina Royalists

With no British presence in South Carolina since the abortive attempt to take Charleston in 1776, Loyalists wishing to serve were forced to make their way clandestinely to East Florida. A large body of these Loyalists made their way to St. Augustine, where they were formed into six companies of infantry and two of horse on May 4, 1778. The corps became an important force in the defense of the province, receiving their baptism of fire at Alligator Bridge on June 30, 1778. They were a part of Gen. Prevost's January 1779 invasion of Georgia, helping capture Sunbury on the 10th of that month. They remained active through 1779, fighting at Briar Creek, Beach Island, Stono Ferry, and the siege of Savannah. In March of 1780 they were a part of Gen. Paterson's column advancing from Savannah to the siege of Charleston. After the reduction of that city, the corps went through a transformation. Many of the original soldiers obtained discharges, replaced by scores of new recruits; 101 enlisted just from July 12 to August 24, 1780. At this time the corps was a part of the garrison of Ninety Six, from which Col. Innes led an expedition on August 19, 1780 into an ambush at Musgrove's Mills, where he himself was wounded. In 1781, the corps was heavily engaged in anti-partisan activities, also forming a part of Rawdon's force at the battle of Hobkirk's Hill. Seeking a major increase in cavalry in the province, the corps was converted almost exclusively to light dragoons in June 1781, eventually reaching a strength of eight troops and one company of infantry. As such they took part in the relief of Ninety Six, the Horse Shoe, the Quarter House and Eutaw Springs. The cavalry formed the bulk of Lt. Col. Benjamin Thompson's corps in early 1782 as he fought against the partisans at Goose Creek, Dorchester, Wambaw Bridge, and Tydiman's Plantation. The corps was converted back to all-infantry and transferred to St. Augustine in October 1782. There they remained until sailing for Nova Scotia in the fall of 1783, where they were disbanded.

2nd Battalion, South Carolina Royalists

Created on February 1, 1779, this battalion was raised mostly from Loyalists who had fought at Kettle Creek, Georgia, on February 14, 1779. Commanded by Lt. Col. Evan McLaurin, the battalion was initially organized into three companies of infantry and three of horse. The battalion never recruited any more than the 169 enlisted men that had originally joined from Kettle Creek. As a result, it was merged into the 1st battalion on October 25, 1779. In August 1780 Lt. Col. McLaurin, who had served as major after the merger, received permission to raise a new 2nd battalion, but it never materialized.

Stanton's Company of Volunteers

An independent Provincial company raised in 1776 by Capt. John Stanton He started the war as captain in the British 14th Regiment of Foot and then became major of the Nova Scotia Volunteers before they went on the Provincial establishment. Stanton in 1776 received a warrant as captain in the Queen's American Rangers, and it is likely his company was likely folded into them.

Stewart's Company of Refugees

Commanded by Capt. James Stewart, this company served in Virginia in 1781, and had probably been raised there that year. Stewart was captured at Yorktown that year, ending the existence of the company.

Stewart's Troop of Light Dragoons

Created on July 9, 1777, this small troop was commanded by Lt., later Capt., William Stewart of New Jersey. Often described as a troop of New Jersey Volunteers, they formed a part of the garrison of Staten Island. Though never more than 25 in number, the troop fought on Staten Island, Elizabethtown, Somerset Court House, Hopperstown, and Pleasant Valley. On July 1, 1781 the troop was made a part of the King's American Dragoons.

Taylor's Independent Company of Provincials

Authorized in 1779 to serve as an independent company of Provincials to be raised at Sandy Hook by Capt. George Taylor. Twenty men were raised for the company, which apparently was disbanded after Capt. Taylor was taken prisoner in the summer of 1780.

Turks Island Company

Raised in 1781 by Capt. Andrew Symmer, the long-serving agent to the West Indian island. With an authorized strength of 61 officers and enlisted men, Symmer believed the company would be quickly raised, as "the Inhabitants are mostly indigent White Men from Bermuda who are enured to the Climate & used to the mode of living & would readily inlist, as when off Duty they may pursue their occupations of making Salt, and being more or less used to the Sea, will when the Service may require their being on board the Schooner, prove very useful Men." The island's only industry was the gathering of salt, mostly for the American market, by slaves. Despite the presence of the small Loyalist force, a black market in salt for America continued throughout the war. After the war, Turks Island was many of the Caribbean refuges that attracted Loyalists, who became cotton planters.

United Corps of Pennsylvania and Maryland Loyalists

Created at Pensacola on December 26, 1779 by the merger of Lt. Col. William Allen's Pennsylvania Loyalists and Lt. Col. James Chalmers' Maryland Loyalists. The corps consisted of six companies, including three of light infantry and one of invalids, commanded by Lt. Col. Allen. Thanks to the personal lobbying efforts by Lt. Col. Chalmers directly to Sir Henry Clinton, the two corps were returned to their former status in December 1780.

Van Alstine's Bateau Company

Raised by Peter Van Alstine of Kinderhook, New York in September 1777, this boat unit went through two incarnations. When raised, Van Alstine and his 26 men joined Lt. Gen. John Burgoyne on his expedition and were part of the force that surrendered after the battle of Saratoga. Under the terms of the Saratoga Convention, Van Alstine and a number of his men later embarked for New York City, where on April 25, 1779 Van Alstine was given command of a new bateau company, this one operating in New York Harbor. In all, 69 officers and men served in the company through the end of 1780, when it was apparently disbanded.

Virginia Horse

A part of Lord Dunmore's Virginia forces, this troop was commissioned on June 7, 1776 and commanded by Maj. John

Randolph Grymes. Raised too late in Virginia to be of any service, it was disbanded on Staten Island shortly after the evacuation of Virginia. Grymes became major of the Queen's American Rangers on September 25, 1776. He resigned his commission 13 months later in protest of the command of the corps being given to Maj. Simcoe.

Virginia Volunteers

An independent company of Refugees serving in 1781 in Virginia, commanded by Capt. Richard Joliffe. He and one soldier of the corps were taken prisoner at Yorktown, effectively ending the unit. Joliffe, owner of a large plantation, served as a spy for Benedict Arnold during his invasion of Virginia. Taken to a jail in Williamsburg, Joliffe soon escaped.

Volunteers of Ireland
also known as the 2nd American Regiment and the 105th Regiment of Foot

Much like the British Legion, American Volunteers and Provincial Light Infantry, this Provincial regiment was created to give an aspiring young Regular officer a command of his own, otherwise unlikely in the British regimental system. Raised by Col. Francis Lord Rawdon in May 1778, the corps quickly raised hundreds of men, both by enlistment and by drafts, principally from the Roman Catholic Volunteers. They and the Queen's Rangers claimed exclusive right to recruit native of Ireland, although this order was largely ignored. Likewise, it should not be thought that only such men were in the Volunteers of Ireland, as they recruited all eligible men who would enlist. In January 1780 the unit was put on the American Establishment as the 2nd American Regiment. The corps took part in Cornwallis' 1778 Bergen County Forage, Gen. Mathew's 1779 expedition to Virginia, the 1779 Hudson River Campaign, the intended 1779 relief of Jamaica, Stirling's Raid on Staten Island, the April 1780 reinforcement to the siege of Charleston, the battle of Camden and Hobkirk's Hill. In the last two mentioned actions the regiment suffered its most severe casualties of the war. In March 1782 Lord Rawdon was authorized to raise a new regiment in Ireland, the 105th Regiment of Foot. The nucleus of this corps would be the officers, non-commissioned officers, drummers, and a few privates of the Volunteers of Ireland. Those men not intended for the new corps were drafted to other Provincial regiments at Charleston shortly before its evacuation in 1782. The 105th Regiment never served outside of Ireland and was disbanded at Downpatrick on January 31, 1784.

Volunteers of New England

The last Provincial infantry regiment raised in the New York City area; only one company was raised. Stationed at Lloyd's Neck, the men served alongside the Associated Loyalists, who garrisoned the post. They assisted in its defense against a French-American force in July 1781 as well as two raids that summer into Connecticut. The unit was commanded by Lt. Col. Joshua Upham of Massachusetts, who served with the same rank simultaneously in the Associated Loyalists. In 1782 the effective rank and file were formed into a troop and joined the King's American Dragoons, in which corps Upham became second major. Onetime aide de camp to commander in chief Sir Guy Carleton, Upham joined Carleton in London in 1783 and became a lobbyist for the partitioning of Nova Scotia to created New Brunswick as a Loyalist province. When that happened in 1784, he was appointed a judge of the new province's Supreme Court.

Ward's Company of Refugees

A small company of independent Refugees commanded by Capt. Ebenezer Ward of Newark, formerly a major in the Essex

County Militia. The company operated from Staten Island the last few years of the war.

Wilcox's Company of Pioneers

This short-lived company was raised during the Burgoyne Campaign. The 25 to 30 Loyalists in the company were commanded by Capt. Hazard Wilcox. The unit's history effectively ended after the Rebel victory at Saratoga. Capt. Wilcox would go on to join James DeLancey's Westchester Refugees, with whom he was killed in action on February 3, 1780 at the battle of Young's House.

A Timeline of the American Revolution

1754

MAY: Lt. Col. George Washington of the Virginia Militia leads Virginia militiamen into territory claimed by the French. His defeat of a French patrol near today's Uniontown, Pennsylvania, is a prelude to the French and Indian War.

1756-1763

The French and Indian War—the North American portion of the Seven Years War—pits Great Britain against France and Indians allied with France; Spain joins France in 1762.

1763

FEBRUARY: Under the treaty ending French and Indian War, Britain gets the Spanish colony of Florida and part of the French colony of Louisiana. The British form the territory into two colonies: East Florida and West Florida.

OCTOBER: King George III restricts the movement of colonists by barring trade and settlement west of the Appalachian Mountains.

1764

APRIL: The British Parliament, without consulting the colonies, imposes its first tax on them: a three-cent tax on refined sugar. The Revenue Act also increases taxes on coffee, indigo, and some wines; it also bans the importation of rum and French wine.

MAY: A Boston Town Meeting protests taxes that "are laid upon us in any shape without ever having a legal representation where they are laid...."

JULY: A fort in Newport, Rhode Island, fires on the Royal Navy warship, HMS *St. John*, in what is regarded as New England's first armed resistance to Britain.

1765

MARCH: Parliament, wishing to pay off Britain's massive national debt following the Seven Years War, passes the Stamp Act, which requires colonists to buy a stamp that is affixed to every piece of paper they use, including legal documents, licenses, newspapers, and playing cards.

Parliament passes the Quartering Act, which orders each colonial assembly to provide British soldiers in America with bedding, cooking utensils, firewood, beer or cider, and candles. A later amendment requires the colonial assemblies to find billeting for the soldiers.

MAY: In his first speech in the Virginia House of Burgesses, Patrick Henry, attacking Britain's treatment of the colonies, says, "Caesar had his Brutus, Charles the First his Cromwell, and George the Third — ." Cries of "Treason!" interrupt him. He pauses before finishing the sentence: "...may profit by their example. If this be treason, make the most of it." He later apologized and stated his loyalty to the king.

AUGUST: A mob protesting the Stamp Act destroys the mansion of Thomas Hutchinson, the lieutenant governor of Massachusetts Colony.

DECEMBER: Boston Sons of Liberty, once members of a secret organization, publicly call for the resignation of the Massachusetts Distributor of Stamps.

1766

JANUARY: The New York Assembly refuses to pay the full amount of money requested by the Crown under to the Quartering Act.

MARCH: Parliament repeals the Stamp Act.

1767

NOVEMBER: Parliament passes the Townshend Acts, urged by Chancellor of the Exchequer Charles Townshend to raise revenue and tighten enforcement of customs laws. Taxes are levied on imported glass, lead, paint, paper, and tea. Another law aids customs officials by authorizing blank search warrants called Writs of Assistance.

1768

FEBRUARY: Massachusetts House of Representatives sends a Circular Letter, written by Samuel Adams, to the legislature of the other colonies declaring that the Townshend Acts were unconstitutional because of a lack of representation in Parliament.

OCTOBER: British soldiers arrive in Boston to aid local colonial officials curb Rebels.

1770

FEBRUARY: A Loyalist, confronted by an angry mob, shoots and kills a ten-year-old boy. Phillis Wheatley, already famed as a black poet, writes a memorial poem and 2,000 march in a martyr's funeral staged by the Sons of Liberty.

MARCH: In a confrontation with a Boston mob, British soldiers kill five people. Son of Liberty leader Paul Revere produces a sensational color print and calls the incident "The Bloody Massacre."

Reacting to the colonists' boycott of British goods, Parliament amends revenue laws, removing Townshend items except tea.

1772

JUNE: Rhode Island Patriots seize and torch the British warship Gaspee, which had run aground while in pursuit of a suspected smuggler.

NOVEMBER: John Adams proposes that the colonies establish a correspondence network to keep everyone informed of political activities.

1773

MARCH: Virginia House of Burgesses creates a Committee of Correspondence and Inquiry that will keep in touch with other colonies about "affairs of this colony ... connected with those of Great Britain." Here, as in other colonies, Loyalists—Tories, as Patriots call them—will not be on such committees.

MAY: Parliament passes the Tea Act, which creates a monopoly. British officials pick Tories in Boston as the exclusive merchants.

DECEMBER: Patriots in Boston dump tea from ships that Sons of Liberty had kept from unloading.

1774

MARCH: Britain closes the port of Boston; other colonies come to the aid of Massachusetts.

JULY: Tories in Worcester, Massachusetts, denounce Committees of Correspondence, charging that their "dark and pernicious" actions were leading people toward "sedition, civil war, and Rebellion."

SEPTEMBER: The First Continental Congress convenes in Philadelphia in reaction to the closing of the port of Boston and other "Intolerable Acts": enlarging Quebec and granting religious freedom to Catholics living there; allowing royal governors to appoint all law officers and have the power to move trials to England; and a demand for expanded quartering of British troops. A delegate with Tory leanings offers an attempt at conciliation, which is rejected.

After British troops seize powder from a magazine on Boston's outskirts, a mob surges into a Cambridge neighborhood called Tory Row. The highest-ranking officer of the colony's royal militia flees for refuge in Boston, starting an exodus. Patriots begin leaving Boston, now a British Army garrison.

OCTOBER: In the first direct action against Tories, the Congress creates a committee for publicizing anyone who violates the nonimportation policies aimed at boycotting British imported goods.

DECEMBER: New Hampshire Patriots capture a fort and seize its arms.

1775

MARCH: Prominent Tories, fearing the rise of rebellious Patriots, ask Gen. Thomas Gates, now both royal governor and commander in chief of British forces in North America, to send a warship to Plymouth Harbor to provide an emergency exit for Loyalists.

APRIL: Firefights at Lexington and Concord pit Massachusetts Patriots against British troops, aided by Tories. As news trav-

els down the eastern seaboard, thousands of militiamen head for Cambridge, beginning the Continental Army.

MAY: Benedict Arnold and Ethan Allen and the Green Mountain Boys capture Fort Ticonderoga on Lake Champlain, acquiring cannon that will be taken to Massachusetts.

The Continental Congress, with delegates from every state but Georgia, names George Washington of Virginia as commander in chief of the Continental Army. He heads for Cambridge.

JUNE: Patriots inflict heavy casualties on British troops in what will be known as the battle of Bunker Hill.

Patriots in Machias, Maine, in a dispute involving a Tory trader, seize a British warship.

JULY: The Loyal Americans Association, first major Tory militant organization, musters in Boston.

The Continental Congress adopts the Olive Branch Petition, which asserts loyalty to the King. He refuses to read the petition and will proclaim that the colonists had "proceeded to open and avowed rebellion."

AUGUST: In a confrontation with Georgia Patriots, Thomas

Brown, a Loyalist leader, is tortured and will raise a vengeful Tory guerrilla band.

NOVEMBER: Lord Dunmore, royal governor of Virginia, issues a proclamation promising freedom to any slave who goes over to the British. Dunmore organizes the Ethiopian Brigade of about 300 African Americans.

DECEMBER: Dunmore, whose Tory force includes his Ethiopian Brigade, leads a battle against Rebel forces at Great Bridge, near Norfolk. Rebels successfully hold the city, driving off British landing parties and sending Dunmore off to in British-occupied New York City.

The Patriots' invasion of Canada, defended by both American and Canadian Loyalists, ends in a failed attempt to capture Quebec.

1776

JANUARY: Tom Paine's *Common Sense*, a call for independence, is published and becomes a bestseller.

FEBRUARY: Patriots defeat a Tory force, led by Scot emigrants, at Moore's Creek, North Carolina, in a major setback for Carolinas Tories.

MARCH: The Continental Army, aided by artillery captured at Ticonderoga, takes control of Dorchester Heights in Boston and begins a siege of British troops.

Gen. William Howe and his troops evacuate Boston and sail for Halifax, taking with them about 1,000 Tory civilians. (See "The First Exiles.")

MAY: Sir John Johnson, Britain's Superintendent of Indian Affairs, and his Tory supporters flee his New York domain, crossing into Canada.

JUNE: Sir John Johnson raises the First King's Royal Regiment of New York. Most recruits are Tories from the Mohawk and Schoharie valleys.

JULY: Congress declares independence, creating an absolute barrier between Patriots and Tories. The first regiment of New Jersey Volunteers, a major Tory military unit, is formed.

AUGUST: British drive Washington's Continental Army from Brooklyn.

SEPTEMBER: Nathan Hale, a Continental Army officer sent to spy on the British, is captured on Long Island by Robert Rogers, who is recruiting Tories for his Rangers. The British hang Hale.

OCTOBER: Benedict Arnold's naval maneuvers on Lake Champlain stymie pursuing British, and the Continental Army's retreat from Canada ends. Tories aided the British along the way.

British capture New York City.

NOVEMBER: A small Rebel force attempts a quixotic and unsuccessful invasion of Nova Scotia, hoping to bring it into the Revolution.

DECEMBER: George Washington crosses the Delaware River and attacks 1,400 Hessians at Trenton, New Jersey, capturing most. He next takes Princeton.

1777

MARCH: The Loyal American Regiment is raised by a leading New York Tory, Beverly Robinson.

JUNE: Gen. John Burgoyne, with the Queen's Loyal Rangers in the advance corps, leaves Canada and begins his two-pronged invasion of New York. His force includes Indians and Tories picked up along the way.

AUGUST: A Tory force of King's Royal Regiment of New Yorkers and Indian allies ambushes Patriots marching to relieve besieged Fort Stanwix in the Mohawk Valley. About 160 Patriots are killed or wounded, as are some 150 Tories.

Near Bennington, Vermont, a foraging force of Burgoyne's Hessians, Indians, and Tories clashes with Patriot militiamen whom Hessian officers mistake for Tories. The Patriots inflict so many casualties that the Mohawk Valley invaders withdraw to Canada, robbing Burgoyne of vitally needed men.

SEPTEMBER: The British Indian Department in New York raises Butler's Rangers, a highly efficient raiding force made up of Tories and Indian allies.

Washington is defeated at Brandywine as British troops march on to take Philadelphia. Tories line the streets to welcome them.

Congress flees Philadelphia and reassembles in York, Pennsylvania.

OCTOBER: Burgoyne surrenders to Gen. Horatio Gates at Saratoga, New York; Tories in Burgoyne's force flee to Canada, where they will join military units.

The victory convinces France to support the Patriots.

1st Battalion of Maryland Loyalists is mustered.

DECEMBER: Washington's army goes into winter quarters at Valley Forge. While Continentals starve, Tory "market people" supply British occupiers of Philadelphia.

1778

JUNE: British troops and a rearguard unit of Tories evacuate Philadelphia, beginning a march to New York. Some 5,000 Tories also leave for New York aboard Royal Navy ships.

Benedict Arnold, military commandant of Philadelphia, begins his betrayal by bargaining with the British through a local Tory.

Washington's army, well trained and better disciplined, emerges from Valley Forge and pursues the British. At Monmouth, New Jersey, the Continental Army mauls but does not defeat the British, as they march to New York.

Virginia Patriots, led by Lt. Col. George Rogers Clark, head west to take territory long held by the British. Clark will capture several British posts in the Ohio Territory (present-day Illinois and Indiana).

DECEMBER: The British begin a southern campaign by taking Savannah, Georgia.

1779

JULY: A British force of about 2,600 soldiers—Regulars, Hessians, and a major Tory unit, the King's American Regiment—makes a series of terror raids along the Connecticut coast, torching and looting New Haven, Fairfield, and Norwalk.

OCTOBER: A joint American-French attempt to retake Savannah ends with the French losing 635 men and the Patriots 457 while the British and Loyalist defenders saved the city at a cost of 55 lives.

1780

MAY: British take Charlestown (Charleston), South Carolina; more than 3,400 Continentals and Patriot militiamen surrender. Troops under Gen. Charles Cornwallis, aided by Tory troops, head to the interior on a campaign to conquer the South.

Gen. Henry Clinton orders expansion of South Carolina Militia, under British Army Major Patrick Ferguson. As many as 5,000 men will join the militia and other Tory units in the state.

Lt. Col. Banastre Tarleton, leading an all-Tory unit called the British Legion, runs into a Patriot force at a place called the Waxhaws on the North Carolina-

South Carolina border. His men kill or wound more than 300 Patriots as their commander seems to be surrendering. Tarleton gets the reputation of a heartless killer called "Bloody Tarleton."

JUNE: Spanish force invades and occupies the British colony of West Florida.

JULY: Loyal Refugee Volunteers, a Tory guerrilla force, wards off an attack on its New Jersey blockhouse by Continental Army General Anthony Wayne.

AUGUST: British rout Gen. Horatio Gates and his army at Camden, South Carolina.

Runaway slaves, recruited by the British, fortify Yorktown and Gloucester.

SEPTEMBER: Benedict Arnold, now in command of the crucial Hudson River fort at West Point, meets with his British case officer, Maj. John André, in a rendezvous set up by a prominent New York Tory. The plot is exposed, Arnold escapes, but André is captured.

British Army Major Patrick Ferguson, who recruits Tories of the Carolinas for his all-Tory American Volunteers, warns "Overmountain Men" that if they do not join him he will march his Tories over the mountains and torch their homes.

OCTOBER: The Overmountain Men round up about 1,400 militiamen, track down Ferguson at King's Mountain on the Carolinas' border, kill him and kill, wound, or capture his 1,100 Loyalists. In the battle—turning point of the war in the South—everyone but Ferguson is an American.

Maj. André is hanged.

1781

JANUARY: Newly commissioned a British general, Benedict Arnold leads his American Legion—1,600 Tories and Continental Army deserters he had recruited—on an amphibious invasion of Virginia. The invaders raid Richmond and occupy Portsmouth after destroying tobacco warehouses.

At Cowpens, South Carolina, Gen. Daniel Morgan leads his Patriots in a classic military tactic known as a double envelopment. They soundly defeat British forces commanded by the hated—and targeted—Tarleton, who gets away.

MARCH: Washington sends about 3,000 men under Marquis de Lafayette to Virginia. He prevents the British from taking Richmond.

At Guilford Courthouse, North Carolina, Gen. Nathanael Greene is defeated by Gen. Cornwallis but inflicts heavy casualties, continuing his strategy to wear down the British.

APRIL: A fleet of 20 vessels carries 7,000 Loyalists from New York City to promised land in Canada.

JUNE: Gen. Greene begins a 28-day siege of a fort at Ninety Six, South Carolina, a Loyalist stronghold held by about 550 Tory troops. As a British relief column nears, Greene withdraws.

JULY: British troops evacuate Savannah. Hundreds of Tories go with them. Georgia, the only colony to be conquered by the British, had reestablished royal militias, which the Patriots must disband.

SEPTEMBER: A joint French and American army under Washington maneuvers to encircle and besiege Cornwallis, who holds Yorktown, Virginia, in anticipation of support from the Royal Navy via the York River.

A French fleet in Chesapeake Bay defeats a British fleet, pre-venting a Royal Navy rescue of Cornwallis.

Benedict Arnold leads a combined force of his Tory American Legion, other Tory units, and British troops on a raid on New London, and Groton Heights, Connecticut. They torch New London and massacre the defenders at Fort Griswold.

OCTOBER: Cornwallis surrenders, ending the last major military engagement of the war.

Tories among Cornwallis' troops slip away, many reaching British-occupied New York.

DECEMBER: British troops, accompanied by hundreds of Tories, evacuates Charlestown (Charleston).

1782

MARCH: Pennsylvania militiamen massacre Delaware Indians—62 adults and 34 children—at the Moravian missionary village of Gnadenhutten, Ohio, in the belief the Christian Indians were Tories.

A mixed force of William Franklin's Associators and Pennsylvania Tories attacks a blockhouse at Toms River, New Jersey, and torches the town. They later hang a Patriot defender, triggering events that lead to Washington's contemplating a retaliatory hanging of a British officer. Ultimately Count de Vergennes, the French foreign minister, intervenes lest the incident affect the war-ending treaty negotiations in Paris.

1783

FEBRUARY: Britain announces an end to hostilities.

SEPTEMBER: The Treaty of Paris is signed by delegates from America, Britain, Spain, France, and the Netherlands.

NOVEMBER: the last British soldiers are evacuated from New York City, along with about 30,000 Tories, who join the Loyalists already in Canada.

1784

JANUARY 14: The Treaty of Paris is ratified by Congress, officially ending the Revolutionary War. By then upwards of 100,000 Tories had left the country.

In Benjamin West's painting of the delegations at the Treaty of Paris, only Americans are visible: John Jay, John Adams, Benjamin Franklin, Henry Laurens, and William Temple Franklin, Benjamin Franklin's grandson, secretary of the delegation. Because the British delegation refused to pose, the painting was not finished.

Index

About the Authors

Thomas B. Allen is the author or co-author of numerous books about military history and espionage, most recently *Tories: Fighting for the King in America's First Civil War*. His children's books for National Geographic—*Remember Pearl Harbor, Remember Valley Forge, George Washington, Spymaster*, and *Harriet Tubman, Secret Agent*, have received outstanding reviews and won multiple awards. He lives in Bethesda, Maryland with his wife Scottie.

Visit him on the web at www.tballen.com

Todd W. Braisted is a long-time researcher of the Loyalist Military, Todd has appeared as a Guest Historian on the PBS Series "History Detectives" and the Canadian Broadcasting Corporation's "Who Do You Think You Are?" He is the co-author of *Moving On: Black Loyalists in the Afro-Atlantic World*; *The Revolutionary War in Bergen County*; and *Revolutionary Bergen County* as well as numerous journal articles. Mr. Braisted has lectured extensively throughout the United States and Canada, before such organizations as the United Empire Loyalist Association, the David Library of the American Revolution, The National Park Service, Historical Society of Pennsylvania, Historic Camden, The Company of Military Historians, and Fort Ticonderoga. He is the webmaster and creator of royalprovincial. com, the leading web site for Loyalist studies. His research has taken him numerous times to such institutions as the Library of Congress, William L. Clements Library, Library and Archives Canada and The National Archives in England. Mr. Braisted has served on the boards of numerous organizations, including chairman of the West Point Chapter of the Company of Military Historians; president, Bergen County Historical Society; president, Brigade of the American Revolution and trustee, 1759 Historic Vought House Association. In 2007, as an acknowledgement of his life's work to date, Todd was made an Honorary Vice President of the United Empire Loyalist Association of Canada, the only American to have ever been so honored. A lifelong resident of Bergen County, New Jersey, Todd currently lives in Mahwah with his wife Susan.

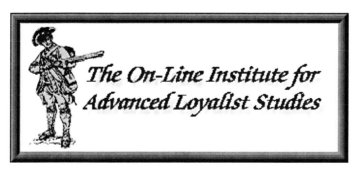

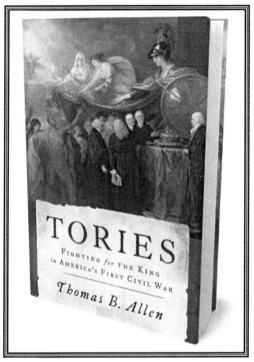

CPSIA information can be obtained at www.ICGtesting.com
232060LV00007B/43/P